Jumpstarters for Meteorology

Short Daily Warm-ups for the Classroom

By
WENDI SILVANO

ISBN 978-1-58037-452-1

Printing No. CD-404093

Mark Twain Media, Inc., Publishers
Distributed by Carson-Dellosa Publishing Company, Inc.

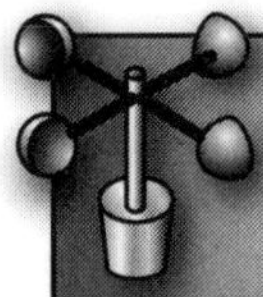

Table of Contents

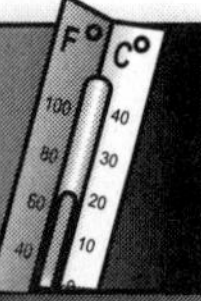

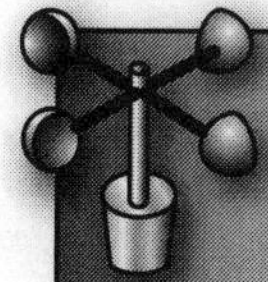

Introduction to the Teacher

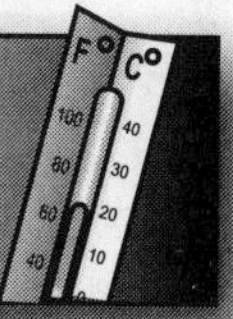

It is important for students to periodically review the information they have previously learned. *Jumpstarters for Meteorology* helps students do just that while also preparing them for the day's lesson by focusing on the topics of meteorology, weather, and climate.

The short warm-up activities in this book provide activities that help students review what they have learned. Each page contains five warm-ups (one for each day of the school week).

Suggestions for using warm-up activities:

- Copy and cut apart one page each week. Give students one warm-up activity each day at the beginning of class.
- Give each student a copy of the entire page to keep in his or her binder to complete as assigned.
- Make transparencies of individual warm-ups, and complete activities as a group.
- Put copies of warm-ups in a learning center for students to complete on their own when they have a few extra minutes.
- Use warm-ups as homework assignments.
- Use warm-ups as questions in a review game.
- Keep some warm-ups on hand to use as fillers when the class has a few extra minutes before dismissal.

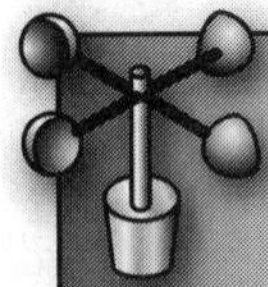

Meteorology Warm-ups: The Atmosphere

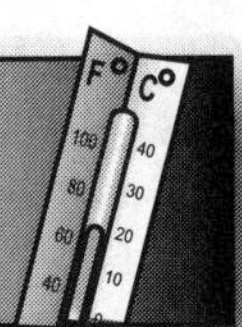

Name/Date ____________

The Atmosphere 1

Write a good definition of atmosphere.

____

____

____

Name/Date ____________

The Atmosphere 2

Write *T* for true or *F* for false.

1. ____ The atmosphere is like a blanket of air surrounding the earth.
2. ____ The atmosphere is over two miles high.
3. ____ The atmosphere retains heat at night.
4. ____ The atmosphere protects us from the sun's UV rays.
5. ____ The air in the atmosphere gets thicker as you go higher.

Name/Date ____________

The Atmosphere 3

Unscramble the names of these things that make up the atmosphere.

1. G N R T O I N E ____________
2. Y N X O E G ____________
3. T R A W E P O V R A ____________
4. R A O N B C I X D I D O E ____________
5. R H T O E S G A E S ____________
6. S U D T ____________

Name/Date ____________

The Atmosphere 4

Number these layers of the atmosphere from the closest to the Earth to the farthest up.

1. _____ Mesosphere
2. _____ Troposphere
3. _____ Thermosphere
4. _____ Stratosphere

Circle the layer of the atmosphere that is split into the ionosphere and the exosphere.

Name/Date ____________

The Atmosphere 5

rotation	unevenly
move	wind
weather	heats

Fill in the blanks.

____________ happens because the sun ____________ the earth ____________. This causes the air and clouds to ____________ all the time. The sun's heat, combined with the earth's ____________, creates global ____________ patterns.

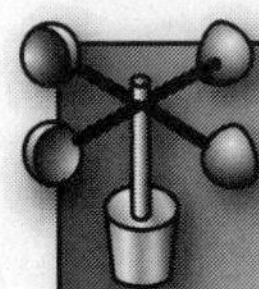

Meteorology Warm-ups: The Atmosphere

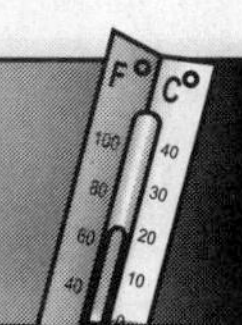

Name/Date ____________________

The Atmosphere 6

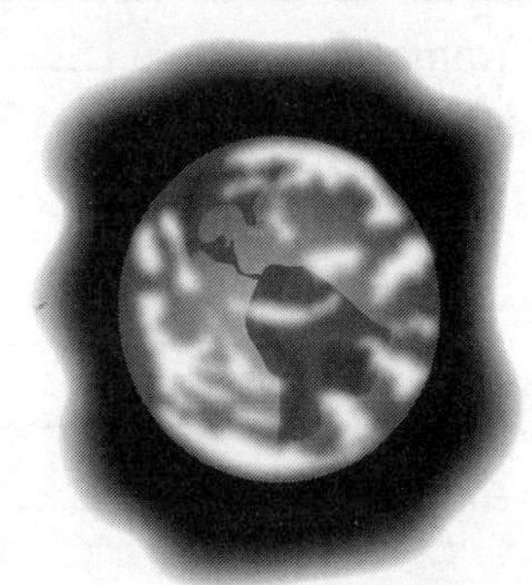

Change the underlined words to make the information correct.

The troposphere is the layer of the atmosphere <u>farthest from</u> the earth. It goes up about six <u>meters</u>. Here is where almost all of Earth's <u>meteors</u> occur. The temperature in the troposphere <u>increases</u> as you go higher up. At the top of the troposphere is an area where the temperature doesn't drop any more. It is called the <u>tropostop</u>.

Name/Date ____________________

The Atmosphere 7

1. Which layer of the atmosphere has most of Earth's weather? ____________
2. Which atmospheric layer reflects radio waves back to Earth? ____________
3. In which layer of the atmosphere do most planes fly? ____________
4. In which atmospheric layer do most meteoroids break up? ____________

Name/Date ____________________

The Atmosphere 8

What layer am I? ____________

Clue one: I begin about 6 to 10 miles above the Earth.

Clue two: My upper layer traps ozone, which protects from the sun's UV rays.

Clue three: Planes like to fly here because there are few clouds or weather to bump them around.

Name/Date ____________________

The Atmosphere 9

summer meteors winter winds mesosphere

Fill in the blanks.

The third layer of the atmosphere is called the ____________. In this layer, there are very strong ____________ that blow west to east during the ____________ months and east to west during the ____________ months. Trails of hot gases left by ____________ can also be seen in this layer.

Name/Date ____________________

The Atmosphere 10

Place a check by each sentence that is true.

1. _____ The thermosphere is the middle layer of the atmosphere.
2. _____ The thermosphere is very hot.
3. _____ The aurora (or Northern Lights) is created in the thermosphere.
4. _____ Satellites travel in the exosphere.
5. _____ Radio waves are reflected back to Earth in the ionosphere.

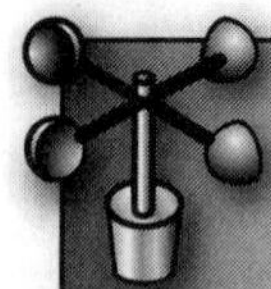

Meteorology Warm-ups: Air Pressure

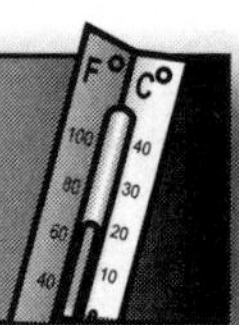

Name/Date ______________________

Air Pressure 1 Fill in the blanks.

amount temperature earth
gravity pressure weight

__________ acts on air and pulls it toward the __________. The __________ of the air being pulled down on an area of the earth is called air __________. Air pressure is affected by two things: the __________ of air above it and __________.

Name/Date ______________________

Air Pressure 2 Write *Yes* or *No* to indicate if each statement is correct.

1. _____ Warm air weighs more than cold air.
2. _____ Air pressure sometimes changes very quickly.
3. _____ The particles in cold air are tighter together than in warm air.
4. _____ Air will move as quickly as it can from an area of high pressure to an area of low pressure.

Name/Date ______________________

Air Pressure 3 Circle which in each pair would have greater air pressure.

1. A beach at sea level — The top of a mountain
2. The equator — The South Pole
3. A cold, snowy day — A hot, sunny day
4. The stratosphere — The thermosphere

Name/Date ______________________

Air Pressure 4 Circle the correct term in each set of parentheses.

1. Although high pressure is caused by (warm / cold) air, it results in (good / bad) weather.
2. Although low pressure is caused by (warm / cold) air, it results in (good / bad) weather.

Name/Date ______________________

Air Pressure 5

1. What did the Italian scientist Evangelista Torricelli invent? __________
2. What does it do? __________
3. Is the instrument he invented the same one we use today? __________

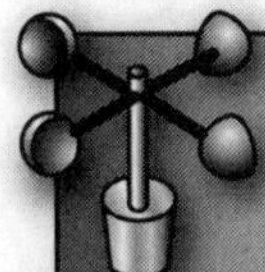

Meteorology Warm-ups: Heat

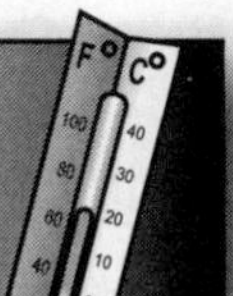

Name/Date ______________________

Heat 1

1. Most of the energy in Earth's atmosphere comes from what? ______________
2. This energy travels to Earth as what type of waves? ______________
3. The direct transfer of energy by these waves is called what? ______________

Name/Date ______________________

Heat 2

Fill in the vowels to complete the names of the three forms in which energy from the sun reaches Earth.

1. v __ s __ bl __ l __ ght
2. __ nfr __ r __ d r __ d __ __ t __ __ n
3. __ ltr __ v __ __ l __ t r __ d __ __ t __ __ n

Name/Date ______________________

Heat 3

Write *T* for true or *F* for false.

1. _____ Infrared radiation is not visible, but can be felt as heat.
2. _____ Ultraviolet radiation has wavelengths longer than violet.
3. _____ Sunburns are caused by ultraviolet radiation.
4. _____ Visible light is a mixture of all the colors in a rainbow.

Name/Date ______________________

Heat 4

What is the greenhouse effect?

____

____

____

____

____

Name/Date ______________________

Heat 5

Fill in the blanks.

ultraviolet	ozone	vapor
scattered	radiated	dioxide
reflected	absorbed	

Some energy from the sun is absorbed by water ______________, clouds, dust, and carbon ______________. The ______________ layer of the atmosphere absorbs most of the ______________ radiation. Some energy is ______________ back into space or ______________ in other directions, and some is ______________ by land and water and ______________ back into the atmosphere.

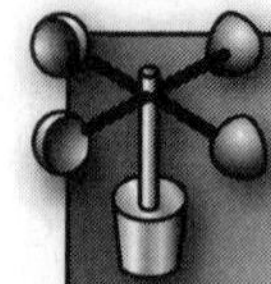

Meteorology Warm-ups: Heat

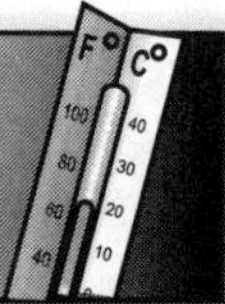

Name/Date ____________

Heat 6

Match.

a. radiation b. conduction c. convection

1. _____ transfer of heat by movement of a fluid
2. _____ transfer of heat from one substance to another
3. _____ direct transfer of energy by electromagnetic waves

Name/Date ____________

Heat 7

Write *T* for true or *F* for false.

1. ____ Cooler, denser air sinks toward the ground, pushing warmer air up.
2. ____ Convection currents move heat in the troposphere.
3. ____ All heat radiated by the sun enters the atmosphere.
4. ____ The atmosphere stops heat from escaping to space.

Name/Date ____________

Heat 8

Using your own paper, explain how the angle at which sunlight strikes the earth affects the average temperatures at areas near the equator and the poles.

Name/Date ____________

Heat 9

Fill in the blanks.

rise sinks movement
slow dense molecules

In hot air, ____________ move faster and farther apart, making the air less ____________. In cool air, molecules ____________, making it more dense. Denser air ____________, making the less-dense air ____________. This creates ____________ of the air.

Name/Date ____________

Heat 10

Air temperature is measured by a thermometer in units called degrees. Two ways to measure degrees are with the Celsius and Fahrenheit scales. Celsius uses the metric centigrade and is used in most countries. Fahrenheit is used mostly in the United States.

Write *C* if a statement applies to Celsius or *F* if it applies to Fahrenheit.

1. _____ A healthy person's temperature would be 98.6 degrees.
2. _____ Water boils at 100 degrees.
3. _____ U.S. weather reports use this scale.
4. _____ Water boils at 212 degrees.
5. _____ Water freezes at 32 degrees.
6. _____ Water freezes at 0 degrees.
7. _____ A nice day would be around 25 degrees.
8. _____ Scientists use this scale.

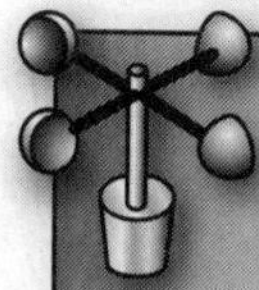

Meteorology Warm-ups: Winds

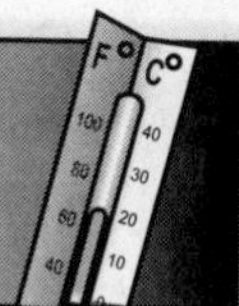

Name/Date ____________________

Winds 1

Fill in the blanks.

1. All surface wind is caused by differences in A____________________.
2. Wind is the horizontal movement of air from an area of H____________ pressure to an area of L__________ pressure.
3. Most differences in air pressure are caused by unequal H____________ in the atmosphere.

Name/Date ____________________

Winds 2

What am I? ____________________

Clue one: I am an instrument to measure wind speed.

Clue two: I have three or four cups mounted at the ends of spokes, which spin as the wind blows.

Clue three: A speedometer attached to my axle will show the wind speed.

Name/Date ____________________

Winds 3

Circle the correct word from each set.

1. The name of a wind tells where the wind is (going to / coming from).
2. A south wind blows (from / to) the south (from / to) the north.
3. Air moves from areas of (higher / lower) pressure to areas of (higher / lower) pressure.

Name/Date ____________________

Winds 4

Use these terms to label the "Earth's Global Winds" chart located on page 34.

Polar Easterlies (use twice)

Northeast Trade Winds

Doldrums

Southeast Trade Winds

Prevailing Westerlies (use twice)

Name/Date ____________________

Winds 5

Which winds are described in each statement?

1. Calm area where warm air rises ____________________
2. These winds blow toward the equator. ____________________
3. These winds blow away from the poles. ____________________
4. These winds blow away from the 30 degree latitudes (or horse latitudes). ____________________

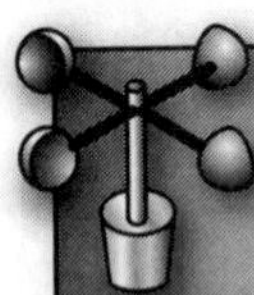

Meteorology Warm-ups: Winds

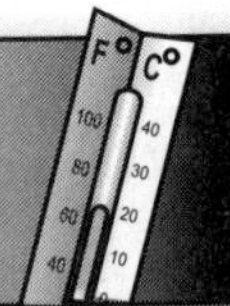

Name/Date ______________________________

Winds 6

What is the "Coriolis Effect"?

____

____

____

____

____

Name/Date ______________________________

Winds 7

How did the trade winds get their name?

____

____

____

____

____

Name/Date ______________________________

Winds 8

Fill in the blanks.

east
high
slowed
west
jet streams
time
fuel

About 10 kilometers above the earth are bands of winds called ______________. These winds are ______________-speed winds that blow from ______________ to ______________. Airplanes traveling in the jet stream save ______________ and ______________ when traveling east and are ______________ when traveling west.

Name/Date ______________________________

Winds 9

Write *T* for true or *F* for false.

1. ______ Unequal heating of land and water that are near each other causes local winds.
2. ______ Water warms up faster than land.
3. ______ Cool air flowing from water to the land is called a "sea breeze."
4. ______ "Land breezes" occur primarily in the nighttime.

Name/Date ______________________________

Winds 10

What am I? ______________________________

Clue one: I am very similar to a sea or land breeze, but over a larger area.

Clue two: I change directions in summer and winter.

Clue three: I bring much needed moisture to South and Southeast Asia.

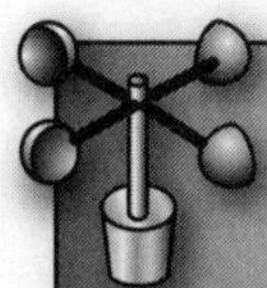

Meteorology Warm-ups: Water in the Atmosphere

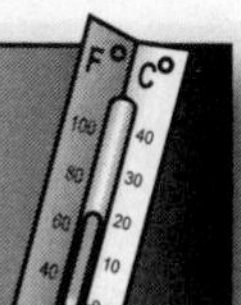

Name/Date ______________________

Water in the Atmosphere 1 List an example of water in each state listed below:

1. gaseous ______________________
2. liquid ______________________
3. solid ______________________

Name/Date ______________________

Water in the Atmosphere 2 Match.

1. _____ The process by which water enters the atmosphere.
2. _____ The instrument used to measure relative humidity.
3. _____ The amount of water vapor in the air.
4. _____ The percentage of water vapor in the air compared to the maximum the air could hold.

a. humidity
b. evaporation
c. relative humidity
d. psychrometer

Name/Date ______________________

Water in the Atmosphere 3 Unscramble these places from which water evaporates.

1. S O E C A N ______________________
2. S L D U D E P ______________________
3. V S L A E E ______________________
4. T S M E R A S ______________________
5. D S N P O ______________________
6. E S A S ______________________
7. I L S O ______________________
8. K S L E A ______________________

Name/Date ______________________

Water in the Atmosphere 4

Why do we feel hotter when the relative humidity is high?

____

____

Name/Date ______________________

Water in the Atmosphere 5 Fill in the blanks.

water vapor, crystals, atmosphere, liquid, condensation, less

Cold air can hold __________ water vapor than warm air. Clouds form when __________ in the air becomes __________ water or ice __________. This process is called __________. When warm air rises into the __________, some of the water vapor forms clouds.

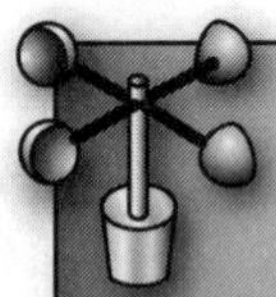

Meteorology Warm-ups: Water in the Atmosphere

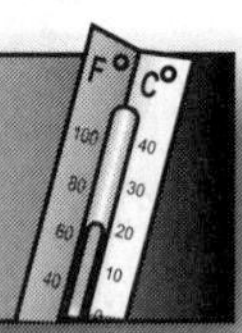

Name/Date ______________________

Water in the Atmosphere 6

Match.
a. frost b. dew
c. dew point d. ice crystals

1. _____ The temperature at which condensation begins.
2. _____ Water condensed on a cold surface.
3. _____ Ice deposited onto a cold surface.
4. _____ Frozen water vapor.

Name/Date ______________________

Water in the Atmosphere 7

Use these terms to label the diagram of the water cycle on page 35. Briefly explain the process of each part.

Evaporation

Condensation

Precipitation

Name/Date ______________________

Water in the Atmosphere 8

Unscramble these sentences about fog and rewrite them on your own paper.

1. clouds that at ground the form near is Fog or
2. dissipates droplets the sun when Fog water the evaporates

Name/Date ______________________

Water in the Atmosphere 9

Give a brief explanation of how clouds form.

____

____

____

Name/Date ______________________

Water in the Atmosphere 10

Fill in the blanks.

condense	rises	clouds
mountain	cools	upward
dew point		

When wind reaches the side of a ______________, the air is forced ______________. As the air ______________, it ______________. If it is cooled to its ______________, the water vapor begins to ______________, and ______________ form.

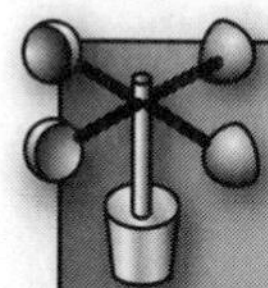

Meteorology Warm-ups: Water in the Atmosphere

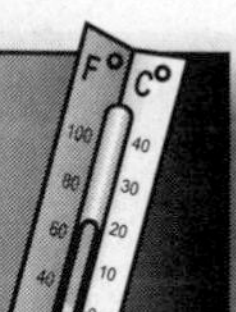

Name/Date ______________________________

Water in the Atmosphere 11

Fill in the missing vowels in the names of these cloud types.

1. C ___ rr ___ s
2. C ___ m ___ l ___ s
3. Str ___ t ___ s
4. ___ lt ___ str ___ t ___ s
5. C ___ rr ___ c ___ m ___ l ___ s
6. ___ lt ___ c ___ m ___ l ___ s
7. C ___ m ___ l ___ n ___ mb ___ s
8. N ___ m b ___ str ___ t ___ s

Name/Date ______________________________

Water in the Atmosphere 12

Match.

a. Cirrus b. Stratus
c. Cumulus d. Nimbus

1. _____ fluffy, heap-like clouds
2. _____ low and gray clouds that bring precipitation
3. _____ high-level, wispy, feathery clouds
4. _____ flat, layered clouds that cover most of the sky

Name/Date ______________________________

Water in the Atmosphere 13

1. Which types of clouds bring thunderstorms?
____

2. Which types of clouds are made up mostly of ice crystals?
____

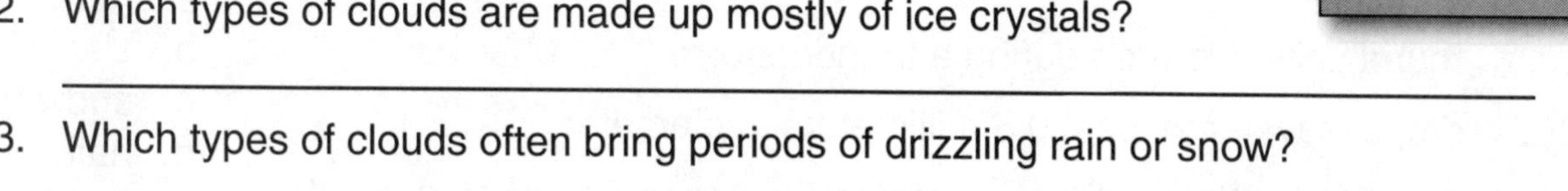

3. Which types of clouds often bring periods of drizzling rain or snow?
____

4. Any cloud that produces precipitation is called this:
____

Name/Date ______________________________

Water in the Atmosphere 14

Fill in the blanks.

droplets	rain	super-dry
vapor	disappear	virga

_______________ is a type of weather that occurs when falling _______________ reaches a patch of _______________ air. The rain _______________ turn back into water _______________ in midair. The droplets seem to _______________ as they fall.

Name/Date ______________________________

Water in the Atmosphere 15

Use these terms to label the types of clouds on the handout (page 36).

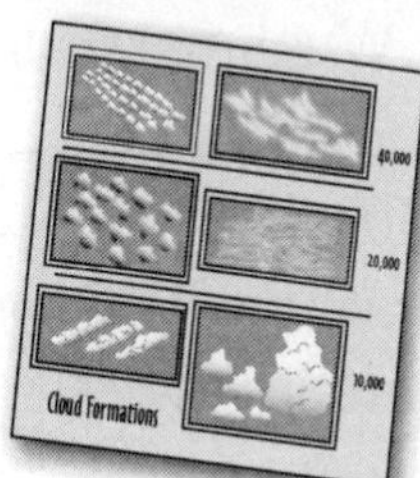

Cirrus
Stratus
Cumulus
Cirrocumulus
Altostratus
Cumulonimbus

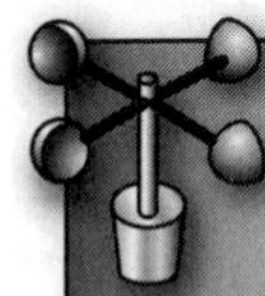

Meteorology Warm-ups: Precipitation

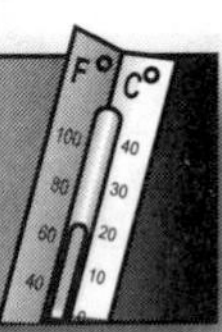

Name/Date ______________________

Precipitation 1

Define precipitation: ______________________

____

Give examples of three types of precipitation.

1. ______________________
2. ______________________
3. ______________________

Name/Date ______________________

Precipitation 2

Write *T* for true or *F* for false.

1. _____ Precipitation always comes from clouds.
2. _____ All clouds produce precipitation.
3. _____ Precipitation occurs when clouds get high enough.
4. _____ Snow is a form of precipitation.
5. _____ Raindrops are smaller than cloud droplets.

Name/Date ______________________

Precipitation 3

Match.

1. _____ drops freeze when they touch a cold surface and ice builds up
2. _____ round pellets formed during a thunderstorm
3. _____ drops of water at least 0.5 millimeters in diameter
4. _____ drops frozen into solid ice particles (less than 5 mm) as they fall
5. _____ water vapor converted directly into six-sided ice crystals

a. rain
b. sleet
c. snow
d. hail
e. freezing rain

Name/Date ______________________

Precipitation 4

1. What is the most common form of precipitation? ______________________
2. Snowflakes are clear. What makes them look white? ______________________
3. What device is used to measure the amount of rainfall that occurs in a particular area at a certain time? ______________________

Name/Date ______________________

Precipitation 5

Fill in the blanks.

ice heavy freeze
hail travel
thunderclouds

______________ forms when droplets of water ______________ around ______________ crystals. These crystals ______________ the air currents in ______________. More droplets freeze onto the crystals, until they become too ______________ and fall to Earth.

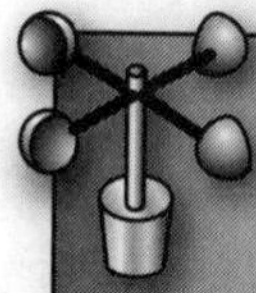

Meteorology Warm-ups: Air Masses and Fronts

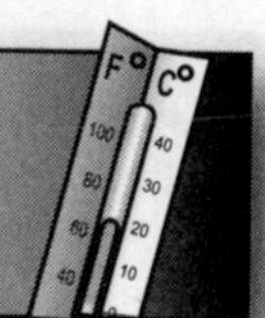

Name/Date ____________________

Air Masses and Fronts 1

An air mass is a huge body of air that has similar air P______________, similar T______________, and similar H______________. It can cover an area as large as one M______________ square kilometers.

Name/Date ____________________

Air Masses and Fronts 2

Unscramble these four weather factors.

1. R A I S P U R E S E R
   ____
2. P M T E U E R T R A E
   ____
3. N D I W R N C T O I D E I
   ____
4. S E T M U O I R
   ____

Name/Date ____________________

Air Masses and Fronts 3

Draw a line to match the air masses to their descriptions.

1.	Tropical	forms over land; dry
2.	Polar	forms over oceans; humid
3.	Maritime	forms over the tropics; warm
4.	Continental	cold; forms north or south of 50 degree latitudes

Name/Date ____________________

Air Masses and Fronts 4

Write *T* for true or *F* for false.

1. _____ Air masses are moved by the global wind currents.
2. _____ Fronts are places where two different air masses collide.
3. _____ Colliding air masses cause storms.
4. _____ Different types of air masses mix easily.

Name/Date ____________________

Air Masses and Fronts 5

List the four types of fronts.

1. ______________
2. ______________
3. ______________
4. ______________

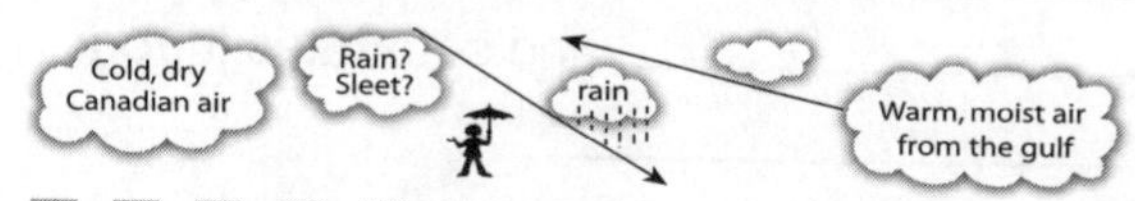

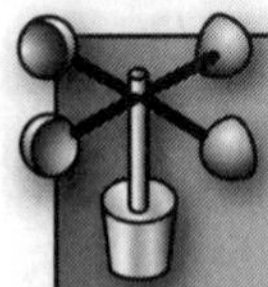

Meteorology Warm-ups: Air Masses and Fronts

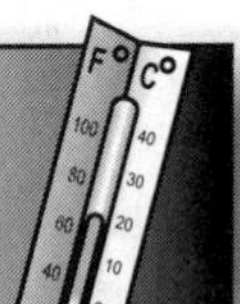

Name/Date ____________________

Air Masses and Fronts 6

Write *Yes* or *No* to indicate if each item about a cold front is correct.

1. _____ A cold front moves quickly and can bring abrupt weather changes.
2. _____ A cold front occurs when a cold air mass runs into a warm air mass and the cold, dense air slides under the warm air, forcing it up and cooling it off.
3. _____ A cold front always brings rain or snow.
4. _____ Cool, dry air and clear skies often occur after a cold front moves through.

Name/Date ____________________

Air Masses and Fronts 7

Circle the word that makes the sentence true.

1. Warm air fronts move more (quickly / slowly) than cold air fronts.
2. The first indicator of an oncoming warm front may be (cirrus / stratus) clouds in the sky.
3. In winter, warm fronts bring (snow / sunshine).

Name/Date ____________________

Air Masses and Fronts 8

1. What type of front forms when two air masses meet and neither one has enough force to move the other?

   ____

2. What kind of weather often results if this front remains stalled over an area?

   ____

Name/Date ____________________

Air Masses and Fronts 9

Fill in the blanks.

upward	occluded	warm
cold	between	ground

An ____________ front occurs when two ____________ air masses come together. ____________ air is caught ____________ them, which forces it ____________ and separates it from the ____________.

Name/Date ____________________

Air Masses and Fronts 10

Write *C* for cyclone or *AC* for anticyclone.

1. _____ A high pressure center of dry air that spins clockwise (in the northern hemisphere), often bringing dry, clear weather
2. _____ A swirling center of low pressure, spinning counter-clockwise (in the northern hemisphere), often bringing precipitation

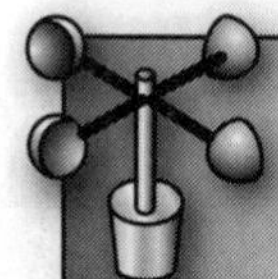

Meteorology Warm-ups: Storms

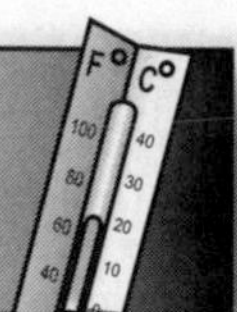

Name/Date ______________________

Storms 1

Circle the word in parentheses that makes the sentence true.

1. Thunderstorms form within (altostratus / cumulonimbus) clouds.
2. Thunderstorms form when warm air (falls / rises) rapidly and cools.
3. Thunderstorms bring (heavy / light) rain and hail.

Name/Date ______________________

Storms 2

Fill in the blanks.

ground	wind shear
updrafts	clouds
burst	spreads

Thunderstorms produce strong ______________ and downdrafts of wind inside ______________. When a downdraft hits the ______________, the air ______________ in all directions. This produces a sudden ______________ of wind called a ______________.

Name/Date ______________________

Storms 3

What am I?______________________

Clue one: I am a sudden discharge of positive and negative electrical charges that build up in a storm.

Clue two: I heat the air to 54,000 degrees Fahrenheit.

Clue three: I kill around 100 people every year in the United States.

Name/Date ______________________

Storms 4

1. Lightning heats the air to a very high temperature very quickly. The air expands suddenly and explosively. What is the sound of that explosion?

   ____

2. Why do we hear the "sound" of lightning a few seconds after seeing it?

   ____

Name/Date ______________________

Storms 5

Check each item that is correct concerning thunderstorm safety.

1. _____ It is safe to be under a tree in a thunderstorm.
2. _____ You should avoid touching metal objects during a thunderstorm.
3. _____ If you are outside in an open area during a thunderstorm, get low and crouch with your head down and your hands on your knees.
4. _____ If you are in a car during a thunderstorm, get out.
5. _____ If you are in or on the water during a thunderstorm, get out as quickly as possible.

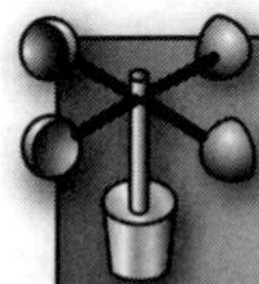

Meteorology Warm-ups: Storms

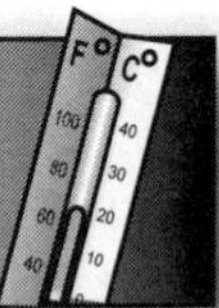

Name/Date ____________________

Storms 6

What is the difference between sheet lightning and fork lightning?

____

____

____

____

Name/Date ____________________

Storms 7

Rewrite the passage on your own paper, correcting the underlined words.

Tornadoes form when <u>cold</u> air is drawn in at the base of a supercell cloud and moves <u>downward</u> in powerful air currents. These warm air drafts begin to spin. If the <u>rising</u> becomes intense enough, the rotating air extends below the <u>top</u> of the cloud as a funnel. If it touches the <u>trees</u>, it is officially a tornado.

Name/Date ____________________

Storms 8

How far away is a thunderstorm? Count the seconds between the flash of lightning and the sound of thunder. Divide that number by 5 for miles and by 3 for kilometers.

1. How many miles away is a storm if there are 10 seconds between lightning and thunder? ____________
2. How many kilometers away is a storm if there are 12 seconds between lightning and thunder? ____________
3. If seconds between lightning and thunder increases, what does that mean?

____

Name/Date ____________________

Storms 9

Write *T* for true or *F* for false.

1. _____ Lightning is always white.
2. _____ You can survive a lightning strike.
3. _____ Lightning rods on buildings conduct electricity to the ground to keep the buildings safer.
4. _____ Hailstones can be as big as baseballs.

Name/Date ____________________

Storms 10

Write *T* for true or *F* for false.

1. _____ Tornadoes are more common in the United States than anywhere else.
2. _____ Tornadoes are the most violent concentration of energy that the atmosphere can produce.
3. _____ Tornadoes occur mostly in the fall and winter.
4. _____ Tornadoes can lift trains off the tracks.

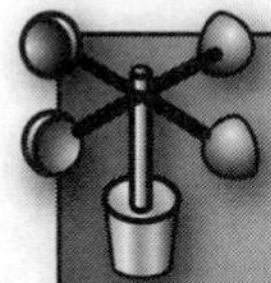

Meteorology Warm-ups: Storms

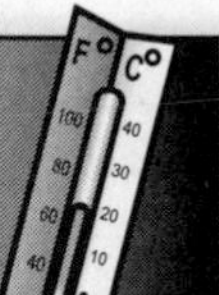

Name/Date ____________________

Storms 11

What is Tornado Alley?

____

____

Name/Date ____________________

Storms 12

Fill in the missing letters.

1. Another name for a tornado is a t _ _ s _ _ _.
2. A tornado that forms over the sea or a lake is called a w _ _ _ r s _ _ _ t.
3. A swirling storm of sand in the desert is called a d _ _ _ d _ _ _ _.

Name/Date ____________________

Storms 13

Circle the correct answer.

1. Which is a more likely speed of the wind in a tornado? 45 mph 370 mph
2. How long do most tornadoes stay on the ground? A few minutes A few hours
3. Why do waterspouts spin more slowly than tornadoes? Water is heavier than air. Warmer air spins slower.

Name/Date ____________________

Storms 14

Match.

1. ____ Which scale is used to measure wind speeds up to 73 mph?
2. ____ Which scale is used to measure the speed of hurricane winds?
3. ____ Which scale is used to measure the wind speed of tornadoes?

a. Fujita Scale
b. Beaufort Scale
c. Saffir-Simpson Scale

Name/Date ____________________

Storms 15

List three interesting facts about tornadoes.

1. ______________________________
2. ______________________________
3. ______________________________

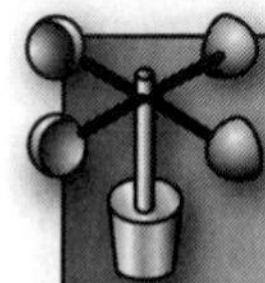

Meteorology Warm-ups: Storms

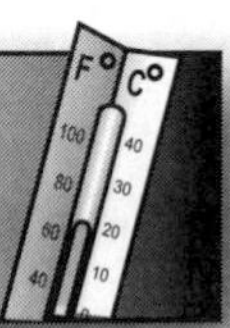

Name/Date ______________________

Storms 16

Write *T* for true or *F* for false.

1. _____ Near the United States, most hurricanes occur between June and November.
2. _____ Hurricanes have winds stronger than 74 mph.
3. _____ Hurricanes are named after the scientist who finds them first.
4. _____ A hurricane's most deadly winds occur in the eye wall.

Name/Date ______________________

Storms 17

Match the tropical storm with its location.

1. _____ over the Pacific Ocean
2. _____ over the Indian Ocean
3. _____ over the Atlantic Ocean

a. Hurricane	b. Typhoon	c. Cyclone

Name/Date ______________________

Storms 18

Fill in the blanks.

winds	land	hurricane
tropical	low	spinning

A ______________ begins over warm, ______________ water when strong ______________ blow into an area of ______________ pressure and start ______________ rapidly. They pick up speed until they reach ______________.

Name/Date ______________________

Storms 19

Number the steps of hurricane formation in order.

a. _____ Winds spiral inward toward the area of low pressure.
b. _____ Wind speed increases until the storm reaches land.
c. _____ Warm, humid air rises, forming clouds.
d. _____ More air is drawn into the system.

Name/Date ______________________

Storms 20

Circle the word in the parentheses that makes each sentence correct.

1. The (lower / higher) the air pressure at the center of a storm, the (slower / faster) the winds blow toward the center.
2. The (highest / lowest) air pressure and the (coolest / warmest) temperatures are at the (center / edge) of the storm.

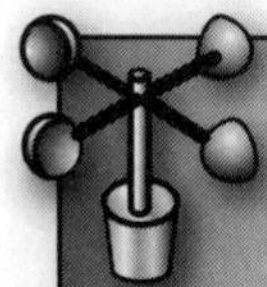

Meteorology Warm-ups: Storms

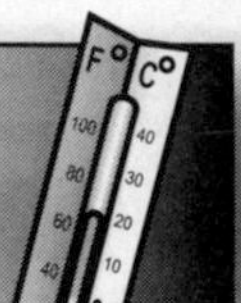

Name/Date ______________________

Storms 21

Using your own paper, compare the types of weather you would find at these places in a hurricane.

1. The outer edges
2. The eye wall
3. The eye

Name/Date ______________________

Storms 22

Fill in the blanks.

strength energy land slow water

When a hurricane hits ______________, it loses ______________ and begins to ______________ because it cannot draw ______________ from warm ______________.

Name/Date ______________________

Storms 23

1. What is the difference between a hurricane watch and a hurricane warning?

____

____

2. Name two preparations to make if you are in the path of an oncoming hurricane.

____

____

Name/Date ______________________

Storms 24

Describe two ways in which meteorologists collect data about hurricanes and their possible paths.

1. ______________________

____

2. ______________________

____

Name/Date ______________________

Storms 25

What is a storm surge and what type of damage does it do?

____

____

____

____

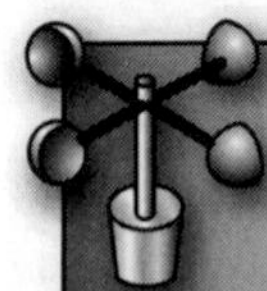

Meteorology Warm-ups: Storms

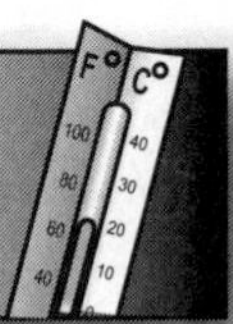

Name/Date ____________________

Storms 26

Fill in the blanks.

condenses	dry
water vapor	snow
lake effect	cools

In the winter, land surrounding a large lake ____________ much quicker than the water. Cold, ____________ air passes over the lake and picks up ____________ and heat from the lake. Then it cools and rises until the water vapor ____________ and falls as ____________. This is called the ____________.

Name/Date ____________________

Storms 27

Write *Yes* or *No* to say if each statement is true.

1. _____ Floods kill more people than any other natural weather events.
2. _____ A broadscale flood occurs when rivers overflow after heavy rain.
3. _____ A flash flood is most likely to happen in the jungle.
4. _____ A barren mountainside is prone to mudslides during heavy rain.

Name/Date ____________________

Storms 28

Match.

a. freezing rain b. icicles c. snowflakes d. hoar frost

1. _____ Water droplets in a cloud freeze to make tiny ice crystals and clump together to form these.
2. _____ Liquid raindrops that instantly turn to ice when they land on frozen surfaces, coating everything in ice are called this.
3. _____ When the surface of snow or ice melts, flows downhill, and then refreezes, it creates these.
4. _____ When water vapor in the air freezes directly into ice on cold surfaces without first condensing into water, it creates this.

Name/Date ____________________

Storms 29

What am I? ____________________

Clue one: I can be triggered by a sudden noise or movement.

Clue two: I can happen when snow builds up in unstable layers.

Clue three: I gather speed as I travel and can create hurricane-force winds ahead of my path.

Name/Date ____________________

Storms 30

Of the many kinds of storms—thunderstorms, blizzards, tornadoes, hurricanes, floods, freezing rain, hail, etc.—which do you consider to be the worst? Why? Write your answer on your own paper.

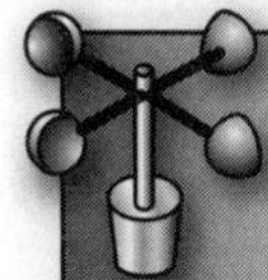

Meteorology Warm-ups: Weather Facts

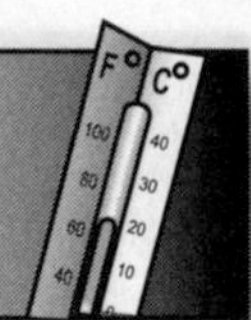

Name/Date ________________

Weather Facts 1

Extremely hot, dry weather can lead to a number of challenging conditions. On your own paper, unscramble the names of these three and then write a paragraph stating why they occur, the effects they have, and an interesting fact about one.

1. G T D U R O H
2. F D I L R W I S E
3. S T D U T M S R O S

Name/Date ________________

Weather Facts 2

rainbows	circle
sunlight	colors
bend	

Fill in the blanks.

____________ are produced when ____________ passes through falling raindrops, causing the light to ____________ and open up the spectrum of ____________ contained in white light. If you saw one from an airplane, it would look like a ____________.

Name/Date ________________

Weather Facts 3

Starting with red, name the seven colors of the rainbow in order.

1. ____________
2. ____________
3. ____________
4. ____________
5. ____________
6. ____________
7. ____________

Name/Date ________________

Weather Facts 4

Identify the bow.

1. A white bow created when sunlight passes through fog ____________
2. A colorful bow created when moonlight hits raindrops ____________
3. A colorful bow created when sunlight hits raindrops ____________
4. A white bow created when sunlight bends ice crystals ____________

Name/Date ________________

Weather Facts 5

What am I? ____________

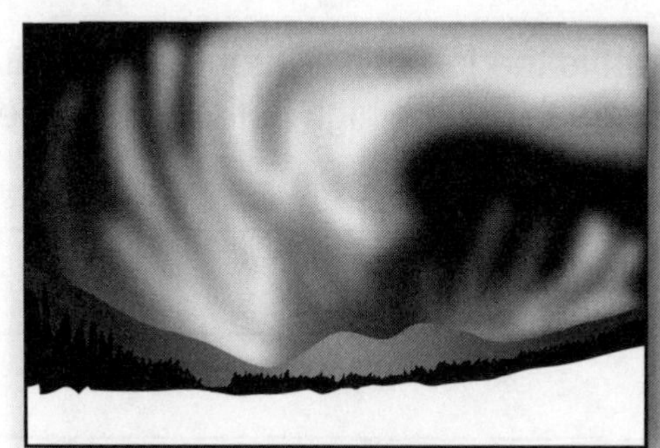

Clue one: I am like huge curtains of colorful light (often green) that wave gently through the skies.

Clue two: You will usually only see me if you are near the arctic regions of the earth.

Clue three: I am caused by the solar wind slamming electrically charged particles into air molecules in the atmosphere.

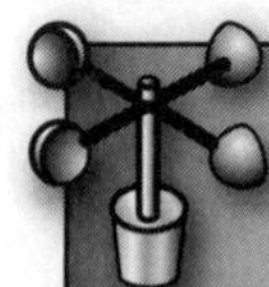

Meteorology Warm-ups: Weather Facts

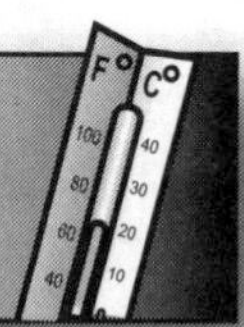

Name/Date ____________________

Weather Facts 6

Fill in the blanks.

South America
humid El Niño
rains Pacific

Every five to seven years, the prevailing winds temporarily change direction over the ____________ Ocean, sending warm water east to ____________. The warm sea makes the air more ____________ and brings heavy ____________ and violent storms. This event is called ____________.

Name/Date ____________________

Weather Facts 7

Circle the effects of El Niño that North America may experience.

violent storms	colder winters
severe flooding	high waves
heavy snow	droughts
milder weather	mudslides

Name/Date ____________________

Weather Facts 8

Match.

a. Mirage b. Brocken Specter c. Sun Dogs or Mock Suns

1. _____ A person's (or thing's) shadow cast on the bases of nearby clouds, which looks like a ghostly figure in the sky, is this.
2. _____ Shimmering reflections that look like water, but are really made when light bends as it passes through air of different temperatures is this.
3. _____ Falling crystals of ice that bend the sun's light produce bright spots that look like another sun on either or both sides of the sun.

Name/Date ____________________

Weather Facts 9

What is the job of the ozone layer that surrounds the earth high in the atmosphere?

____

____

____

Name/Date ____________________

Weather Facts 10

Write *T* for true or *F* for false.

1. _____ Ozone forms in the stratosphere.
2. _____ Without enough ozone, more people will get skin cancer.
3. _____ Man-made chemicals destroy ozone.
4. _____ Ozone holes are over North America.
5. _____ At ground level, ozone is a type of pollution.

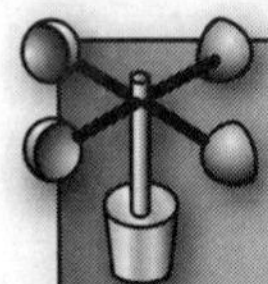

Meteorology Warm-ups: Predicting the Weather

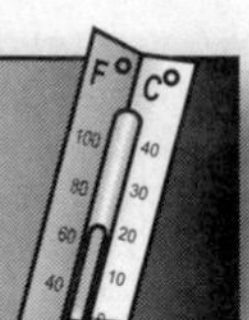

Name/Date ______________________

Predicting the Weather 1

Write *T* for true or *F* for false.

1. _____ Weather balloons travel in the exosphere.
2. _____ A weather balloon's drift shows wind speed and direction.
3. _____ When a balloon pops, the instruments crash into the ground.
4. _____ A weather balloon carries a box of measuring equipment.
5. _____ Hundreds of weather balloons are released around the world each day.

Name/Date ______________________

Predicting the Weather 2

What three things do weather balloons measure?

1. A______________________
2. H______________________
3. T______________________

Name/Date ______________________

Predicting the Weather 3

Draw a line to connect each of these weather instruments with what they measure.

1. barometer	temperature
2. psychrometer	wind speed
3. thermometer	relative humidity
4. anemometer	wind direction
5. wind vane	air pressure

Name/Date ______________________

Predicting the Weather 4

How do satellites help in weather prediction?

____

____

____

____

____

Name/Date ______________________

Predicting the Weather 5

Fill in the blanks.

data
currents
buoys
satellites
tracking

Weather ______________ float on the surface of the oceans. They carry transmitters that beam weather ______________ to ______________. Important information is also gained by ______________ the buoys as they are carried along by ocean ______________.

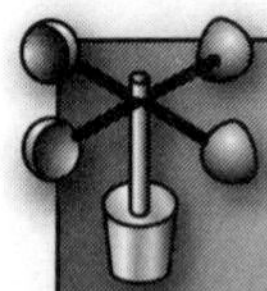

Meteorology Warm-ups: Predicting the Weather

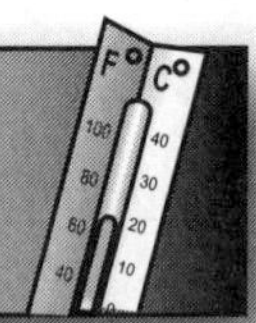

Name/Date ____________________

Predicting the Weather 6

From which four sources do meteorologists get weather information?

1. ____________________ 2. ____________________

3. ____________________ 4. ____________________

Name/Date ____________________

Predicting the Weather 7

What am I? ____________________

Clue one: I am used to track weather balloons in flight.

Clue two: I am a technology that helps track rainfall, storms, wind speed, and cloud positions.

Clue three: I work by sending out short radio waves that are reflected back.

Name/Date ____________________

Predicting the Weather 8 Label the weather instruments on page 37.

thermometer	rain gauge	psychrometer
anemometer	wind vane	hygrometer
mercury barometer	weather balloon	aneroid barometer

Name/Date ____________________

Predicting the Weather 9 Fill in the blanks.

predict space millions
analyze supercomputers

Information from weather stations is fed into ____________________, which ____________________ data from land, sea, air, and ____________________. They can perform ____________________ of calculations, which allows them to ____________________ how the weather will change.

Name/Date ____________________

Predicting the Weather 10

Buoys carry weather stations on the oceans. Why is it important to monitor weather conditions at sea?

____

____

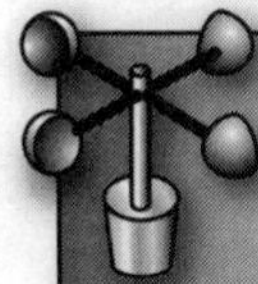

Meteorology Warm-ups: Predicting the Weather

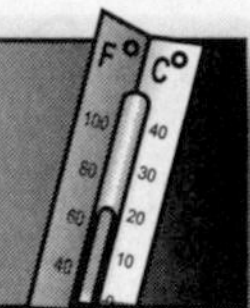

Name/Date ______

Predicting the Weather 11

Write *Yes* or *No* to indicate if each statement is correct.

1. _____ A weather map is a "snapshot" of weather conditions over a large area.
2. _____ There are many different types of weather maps.
3. _____ The National Weather Service produces many weather maps.
4. _____ Isotopes on weather maps connect places with similar temperatures.

Name/Date ______

Predicting the Weather 12

List four things that might be indicated on a weather map.

1. ______
2. ______
3. ______
4. ______

Name/Date ______

Predicting the Weather 13

What is the difference between an isobar and an isotherm?

______

______

______

______

Name/Date ______

Predicting the Weather 14

What type of front does each of these symbols represent?

______ ______

______ ______

Name/Date ______

Predicting the Weather 15

Label these weather map symbols using the handout on page 38.

drizzle	fog	hail
haze	rain	shower
sleet	smoke	snow
thunderstorm		hurricane

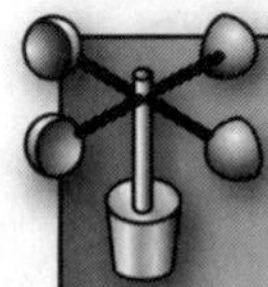

Meteorology Warm-ups: Predicting the Weather

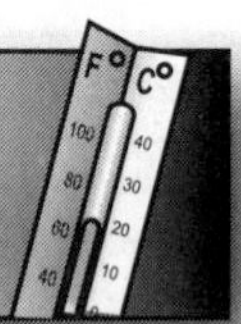

Name/Date ______________________

Predicting the Weather 16

Match the weather map symbol with the conditions it would indicate.

a.

b.

c.

1. _____ Winds from the northeast with speeds of 67 to 71 mph with 20–30% cloud cover.

2. _____ Winds from the southwest with speeds of 9 to 14 miles per hour with 100% cloud cover.

3. _____ Winds from the northwest with speeds of 44 to 49 miles per hour with 50% cloud cover.

Name/Date ______________________

Predicting the Weather 17

precipitation	fronts
temperatures	
pressure	cloud

Fill in the blanks.

Weather maps often show predicted ______________, chances of sun or ______________ cover, and locations of rain or snow ______________. They may include symbols for warm or cold ______________ and high or low ______________ areas.

Name/Date ______________________

Predicting the Weather 18

Use the weather map on page 39 to answer these questions.

1. What kind of weather is Denver, Colorado, experiencing?
2. Name one city that is in a high-pressure area.
3. Name one city that is in a low-pressure area.
4. How many different types of fronts are on the map?
5. Can you tell what season it is? How?

Name/Date ______________________

Predicting the Weather 19

List two things that would be on a weather map of your area today.

1. ______________________
2. ______________________

Name/Date ______________________

Predicting the Weather 20

1. What do meteorologists call their weather maps?

   ____

2. Why do they use symbols instead of words to indicate information? ______________________

   ____

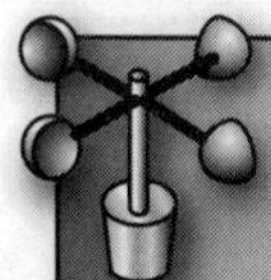

Meteorology Warm-ups: Weather Myths and Folklore

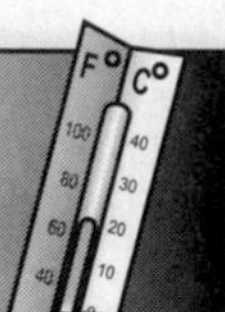

Name/Date ______________________

Weather Myths and Folklore 1

Draw lines to match the folklore phrases about weather.

1. Clear moon,	a year of plenty.
2. Red sky at night,	the nearer the rain.
3. Red sky in morning,	frost soon.
4. Rainbow in morning	sailor take warning.
5. A year of snow,	sailor's delight.
6. The farther the sight,	gives you fair warning.

Name/Date ______________________

Weather Myths and Folklore 2

Write *T* for true or *F* for false.

1. ____ Opening windows before a tornado hits equalizes the pressure.
2. ____ The low air pressure around a tornado causes buildings to explode.
3. ____ It is safer to get into a ditch during a tornado than to stay in your car.
4. ____ Tornadoes never occur downtown.

Name/Date ______________________

Weather Myths and Folklore 3

Match.

a. Huracan b. Thor
c. Poseidon d. Ra

1. _____ I am the Viking god of thunder.
2. _____ I am the Egyptian god of the sun.
3. _____ I am the Mayan god of creation for whom hurricanes were named.
4. _____ I am the Greek god of the sea and waves.

Name/Date ______________________

Weather Myths and Folklore 4

One traditional way to tell of an approaching storm was to hang seaweed. If it stayed slimy, rain was predicted. Why do you think this worked?

____

____

____

Name/Date ______________________

Weather Myths and Folklore 5

red ring squirrel's
thunderstorm cows

Many early civilizations believed weather myths like these, which may have some truth to them. Fill in the blanks with words from the list.

1. When ______________ are lying down, there will be rain.
2. Roosters crow more before a ______________.
3. The bushier a ______________ tail is in fall, the harsher the coming winter will be.
4. A ______________ sky in the morning means a coming storm.
5. A ______________ around the moon means there will be rain.

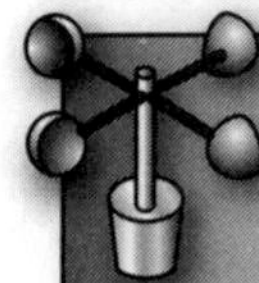

Meteorology Warm-ups: Climate

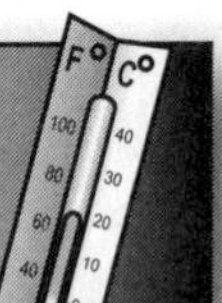

Name/Date ______

Climate 1

Write a good definition of climate.

______

______
______
______
______
______

Name/Date ______

Climate 2

What are the two main factors that determine the climate of a region?

1. ______

2. ______

Name/Date ______

Climate 3

Fill in the missing vowels in the names of these factors that influence temperature.

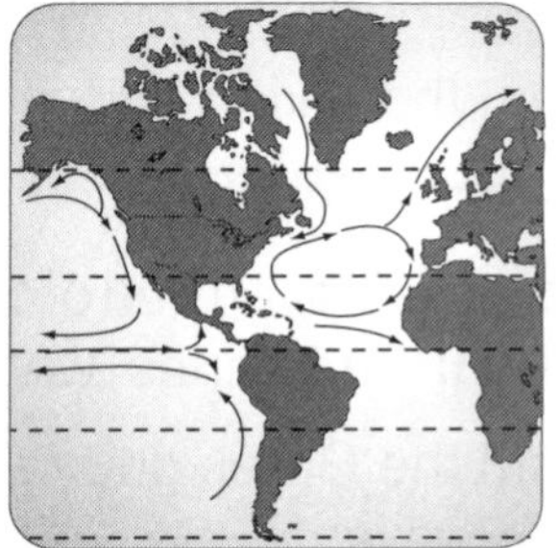

1. L __ t __ t __ d __
2. __ lt __ t __ d __
3. D __ st __ nc __ fr __ m l __ rg __ b __ d __ __ s __ f w __ t __ r
4. __ c __ __ n c __ rr __ nts

Name/Date ______

Climate 4

Latitude distances divide the Earth into three temperature zones. What are they? Describe the temperatures in each in a few words.

1. ______
2. ______
3. ______

Name/Date ______

Climate 5

Fill in the blanks.

tropical	mountains
cooler	altitude
temperature	

One of the most important factors of ______ on top of high ______ is ______. Very high areas everywhere have ______ temperatures, even those in the ______ zone.

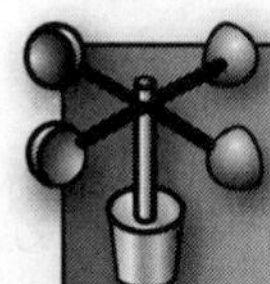

Meteorology Warm-ups: Climate

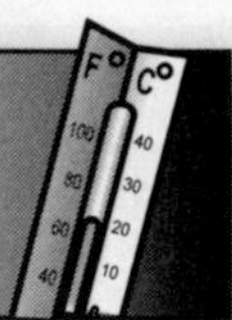

Name/Date ______________________

Climate 6

Circle one word in parentheses to make the sentence true.

1. Oceans make the temperatures of nearby land (more / less) extreme.
2. Water heats up and cools down (more / less) slowly than land.
3. Most coastal climates are more (mild / extreme) than inland areas.

Name/Date ______________________

Climate 7

tropics	equator	land
currents	poles	

Fill in the blanks.

Ocean ____________ move in regular patterns. Warm currents carry warm water from the ____________ to the poles. Cold currents carry cold water from the ____________ toward the ____________. The warm or cool air carries over to nearby ____________.

Name/Date ______________________

Climate 8

What are two main factors that affect precipitation?

1. ______________________
2. ______________________

Name/Date ______________________

Climate 9

1. What moves the huge air masses in the atmosphere?
____
2. What in the air affects how much rain or snow will fall?
____
3. Does warm air or cold air hold more water vapor?
____

Name/Date ______________________

Climate 10

List each item under the correct climate.

cool summers
warm winters
hot summers
cold winters
inland areas
coastal areas
more temperature variation
less temperature variation

Marine climates

____
____
____
____

Continental climates

____
____
____
____

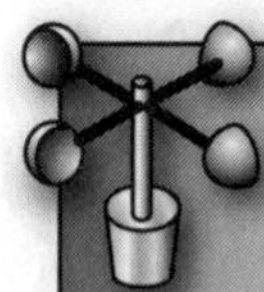

Meteorology Warm-ups: Climate

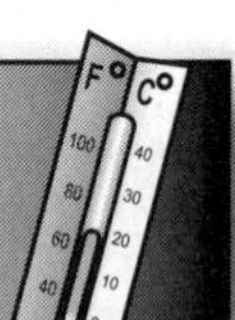

Name/Date ______________________

Climate 11

Fill in the blanks.

Atlantic
toward
Sahara
Asia
Mediterranean
dry

Even though the ____________ Desert is near both the ____________ Sea and the ____________ Ocean, it is extremely ____________ because the winds that blow ____________ this area come from inland ____________ and carry little water vapor.

Name/Date ______________________

Climate 12

Circle the word that makes the sentence true.

1. The (windward / leeward) side of a mountain gets more precipitation.
2. When humid winds reach a mountain, they rise, the air (cools / warms), and the water vapor (evaporates / condenses).
3. By the time air reaches the leeward side of a mountain, it is usually cool and (dry / wet).

Name/Date ______________________

Climate 13

What is a microclimate?

____

____

____

____

Name/Date ______________________

Climate 14

1. The seasons are caused by the ____________ of the earth's ____________.
2. The axis of the earth always points toward the ____________.
3. Earth rotates on its own axis once every ____________.

Name/Date ______________________

Climate 15

Write *T* for true or *F* for false.

1. _____ The Northern and Southern Hemispheres have opposite seasons.
2. _____ In June, Canada receives more direct sunlight than Brazil.
3. _____ Days are shorter in December in the Southern Hemisphere.
4. _____ In the spring and fall, neither end of Earth's axis is tilted toward the sun.

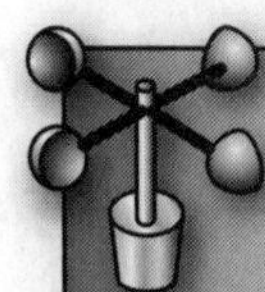

Meteorology Warm-ups: Climate

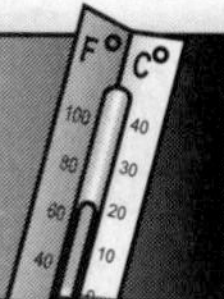

Name/Date ____________________

Climate 16

Fill in the missing letters to complete the five climate regions.

1. __ r __ __ __ c __ __
2. D __ __
3. T __ __ p __ __ a __ e M __ r __ n __
4. __ em __ __ r __ te C __ nt __ n __ __ t __ l
5. P __ __ __ __ __

Name/Date ____________________

Climate 17

1. What kind of forest would you find in a tropical climate? ____________
2. Describe a tropical wet climate. ____________ ____________
3. In tropical wet climates, it r __ __ __ s almost every day in the a __ __ __ r __ __ __ n.

Name/Date ____________________

Climate 18

1. How is a tropical wet-and-dry climate different from a tropical wet climate? ____________ ____________
2. Most of the areas with tropical rainy climates are near the e __ __ __ __ __ __ __.

Name/Date ____________________

Climate 19

Fill in the blanks.

dry hotter rainfall precipitation evaporate

If the amount of ____________ that falls is less than the amount of water that could potentially ____________, a climate is considered ____________. A cooler area with low ____________ would not be as dry as a ____________ place with the same amount of rain.

Name/Date ____________________

Climate 20

The five climate regions are subdivided. Put these climates under their primary climate region.

Tundra	Mediterranean
Semiarid	Humid continental
Arid	Marine west coast
Ice cap	Humid subtropical
Subarctic	Tropical wet
Tropical wet-and-dry	

Tropical

____

____

Dry

____

____

Temperate Marine

____

____

____

Temperate Continental

____

____

Polar

____

____

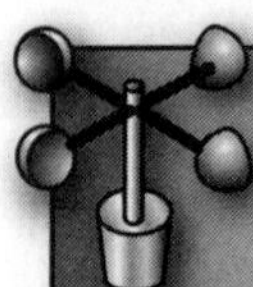

Meteorology Warm-ups: Climate

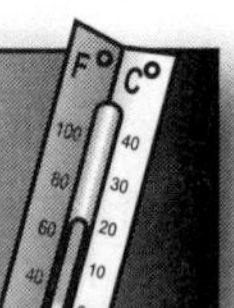

Name/Date ____________________

Climate 21

Write *T* for true or *F* for false.

1. ______ All deserts are hot and sandy.
2. ______ Plants that grow well in arid climates are yucca and cactus.
3. ______ Arid regions get an average of about 10 inches of rain per year.
4. ______ In deserts, it is hot both day and night.
5. ______ The Arctic is classified as a desert.

Name/Date ____________________

Climate 22

Fill in the vowels of these four large deserts found in the United States.

1. Ch __ h __ __ h __ __ n D __ s __ rt
2. Gr __ __ t B __ s __ n D __ s __ rt
3. M __ j __ v __ D __ s __ rt
4. S __ n __ r __ n D __ s __ rt

Name/Date ____________________

Climate 23

1. The Great Plains of the United States is a semiarid climate. Why is that good for raising livestock, such as cattle, sheep, and goats?

   ____

2. Name two crops that grow well in this type of climate.

   a. ____________________

   b. ____________________

Name/Date ____________________

Climate 24

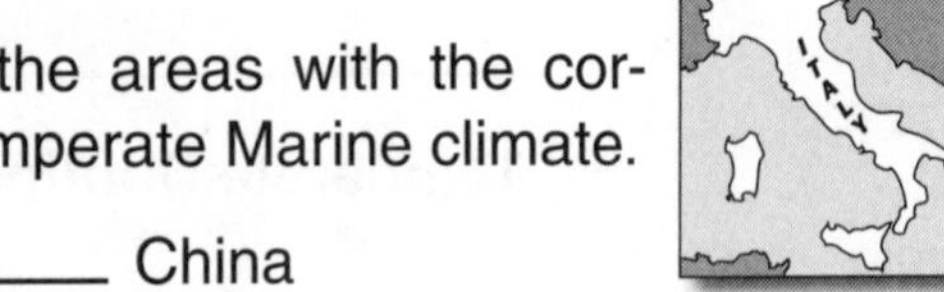

Match the areas with the correct Temperate Marine climate.

1. ______ China
2. ______ Italy and Greece
3. ______ U.S. Pacific Northwest

a. Mediterranean b. Humid subtropical
c. Marine west coast

Name/Date ____________________

Climate 25

Which Temperate Marine climate has:

1. Warm, dry summers and cool, rainy winters? ____________________
2. Hot summers and cool winters?

   ____

3. Moderate precipitation year round, with mild winters and cool summers?

   ____

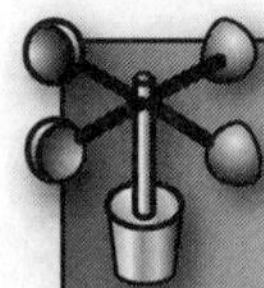

Meteorology Warm-ups: Climate

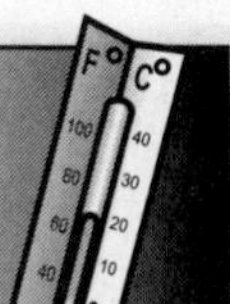

Name/Date ____________________

Climate 26

Write *T* for true and *F* for false.

1. ______ Temperate continental climates are only in the Northern Hemisphere.
2. ______ Temperate continental climates have temperature extremes.
3. ______ The southeastern United States has a humid continental climate.
4. ______ Northern Russia and Canada have subarctic climates.

Name/Date ____________________

Climate 27

Match the temperate continental climate to its description.

1. ____ Long, cold winters and short, cool summers with light precipitation
2. ____ Hot, wet summers and cold winters with moderate precipitation

a. humid continental b. subarctic

Name/Date ____________________

Climate 28

Fill in the blanks.

Canada
animals
trees
tundra
cool
cold
permafrost

The ____________ climate region is found in northern Russia, ____________, and Alaska. It has bitterly ____________ winters and short, ____________ summers. Some layers of soil in the tundra never thaw. This is called ____________. It is too cold for ____________ to grow on the tundra, but many ____________ live there.

Name/Date ____________________

Climate 29

What climate region am I? ____________

Clue one: My average temperatures are always at or below freezing.

Clue two: All land in my region is covered with ice and snow.

Clue three: My air is very dry.

Name/Date ____________________

Climate 30

The Highlands are a distinct climate region. Match these highland areas with similar climate.

1. ______ Lower slopes of a mountain range
2. ______ Higher up the mountain, but not the top
3. ______ Above the tree line—top section

a. similar to a subarctic zone
b. similar to the tundra
c. similar to surrounding area

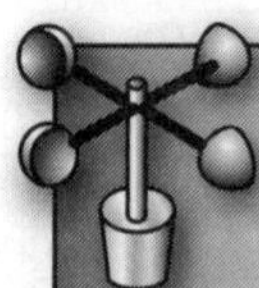

Meteorology Warm-ups: Earth's Global Winds

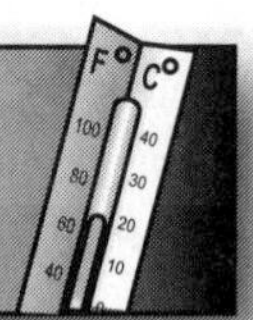

Label the diagram with the terms from Winds 4 on page 7.

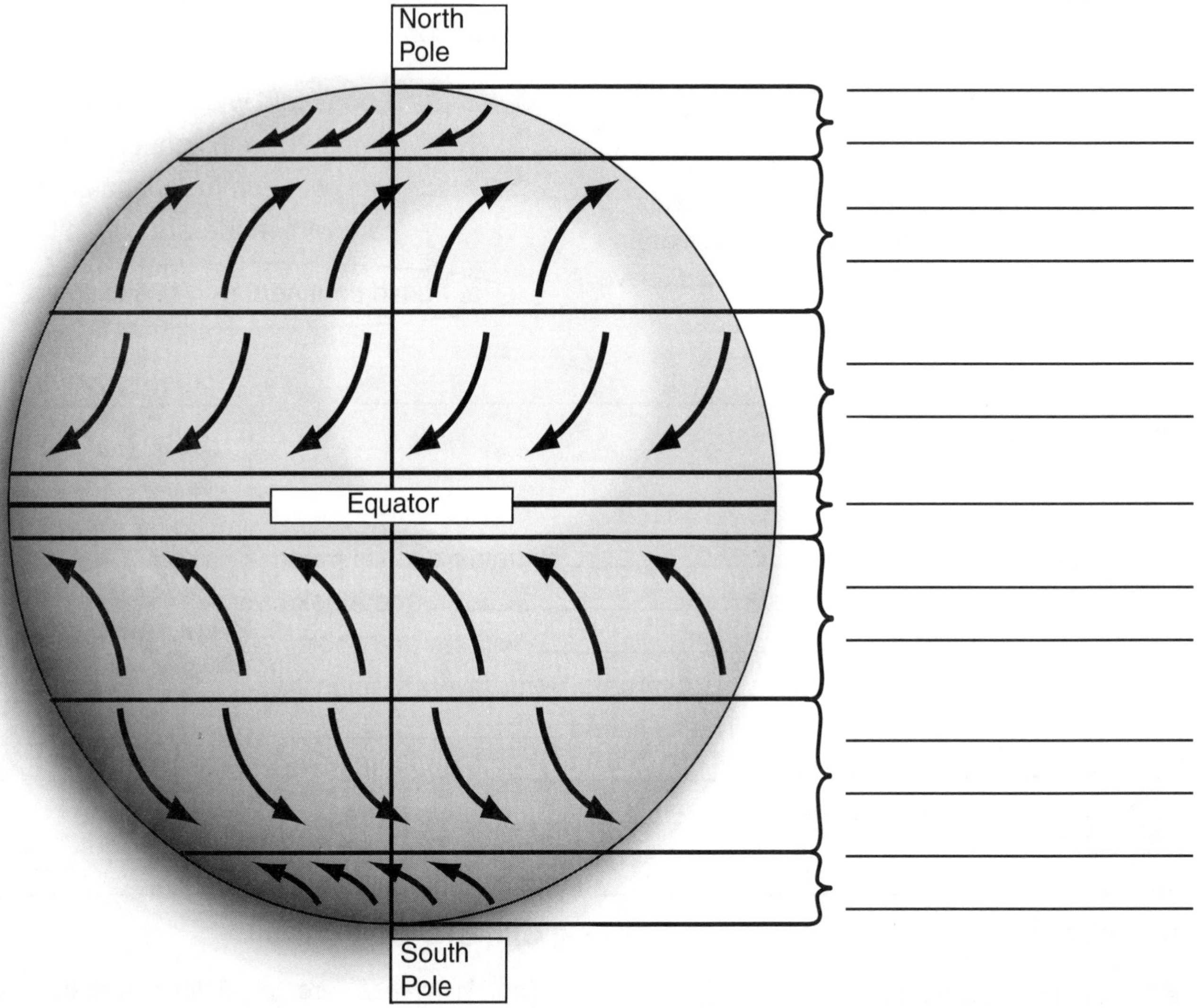

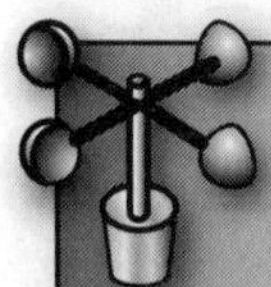

Meteorology Warm-ups: Water Cycle

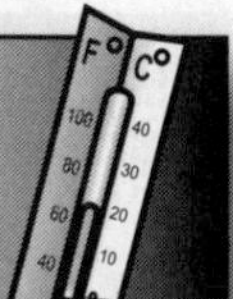

Label the diagram with the terms from Water in the Atmosphere 7 on page 10.

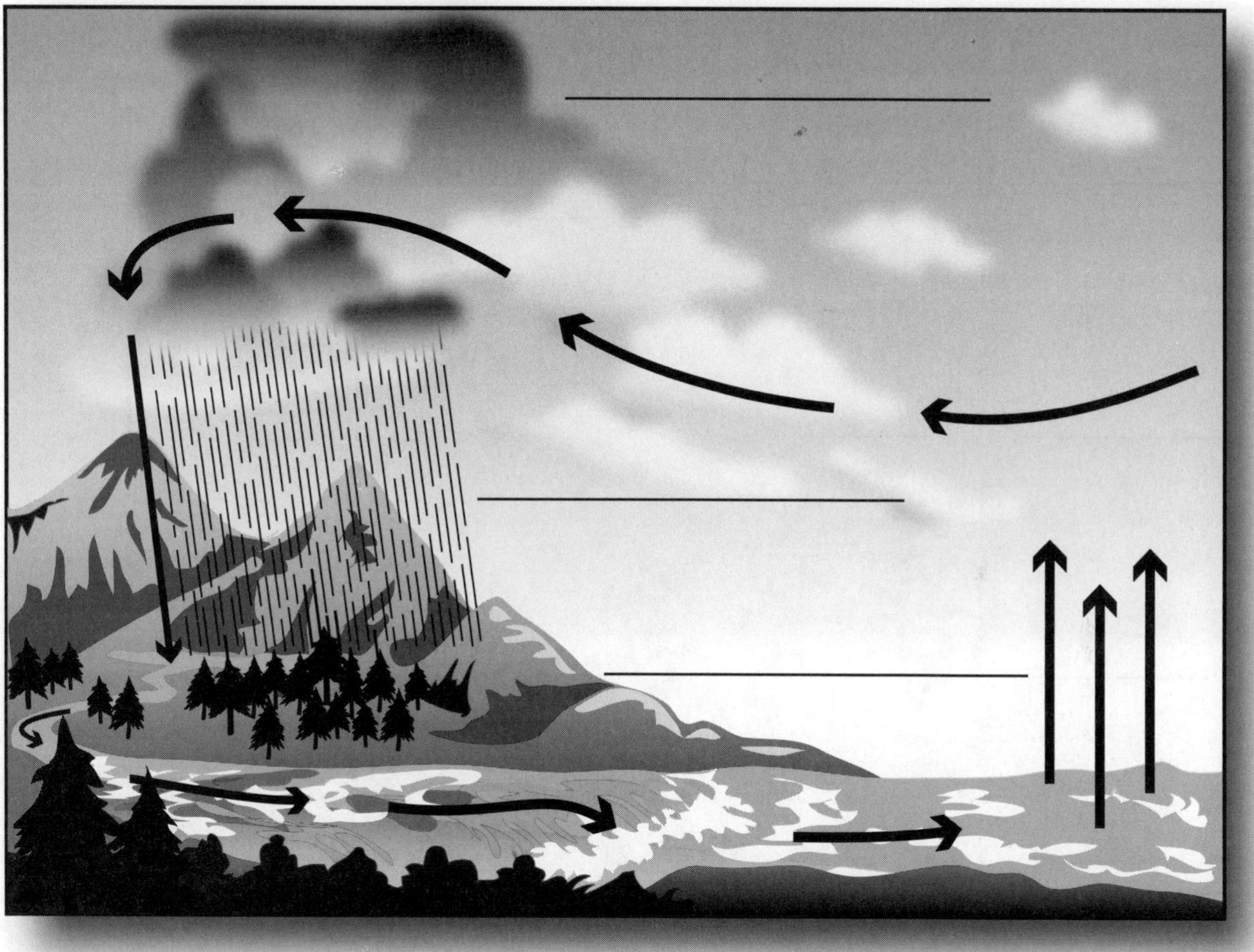

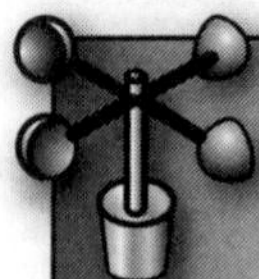

Meteorology Warm-ups: Cloud Types

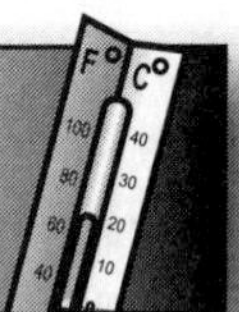

Label the diagram with the terms from Water in the Atmosphere 15 on page 11.

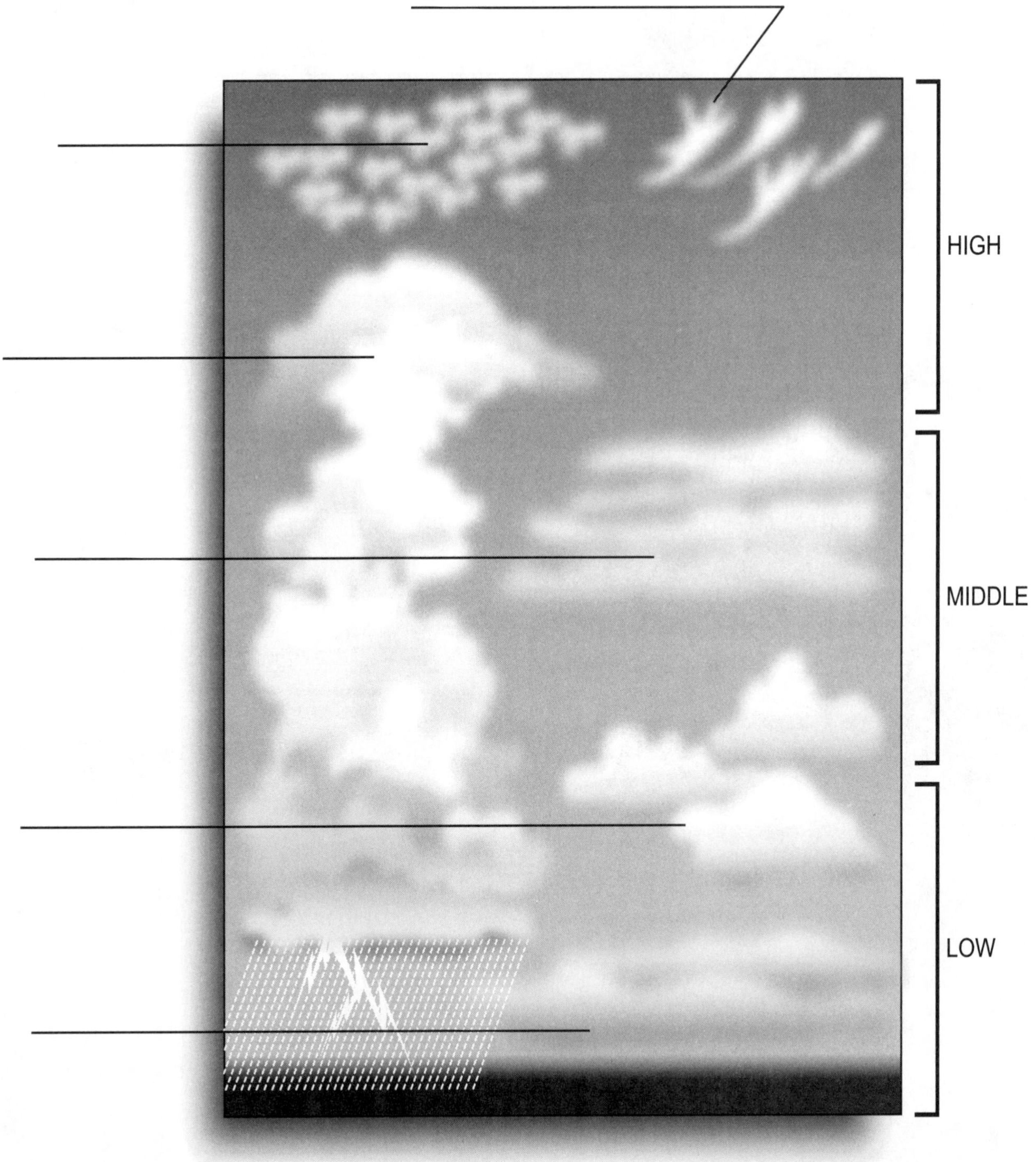

HIGH

MIDDLE

LOW

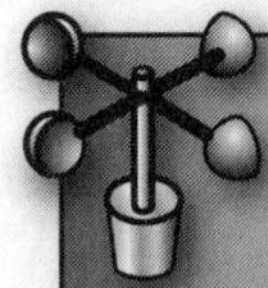

Meteorology Warm-ups: Weather Instruments

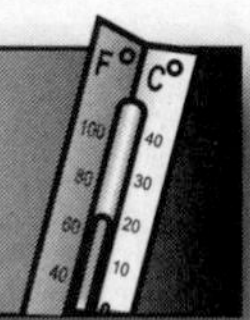

Label the pictures with the correct instrument names from Predicting the Weather 8 on page 24.

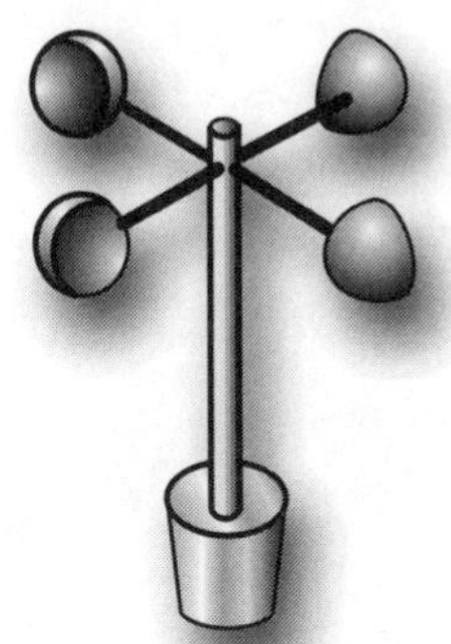

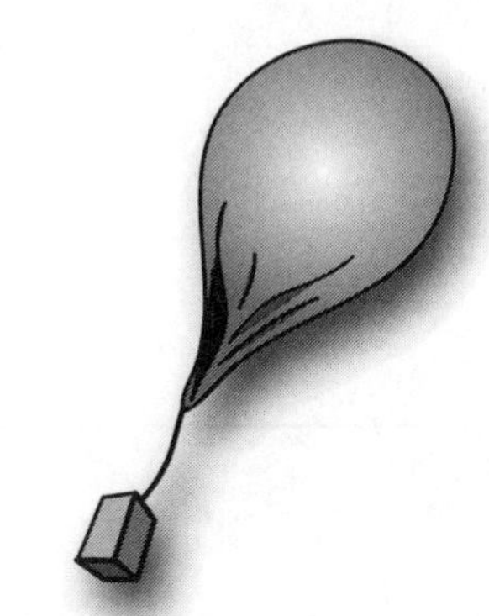

1. ____________________ 2. ____________________ 3. ____________________

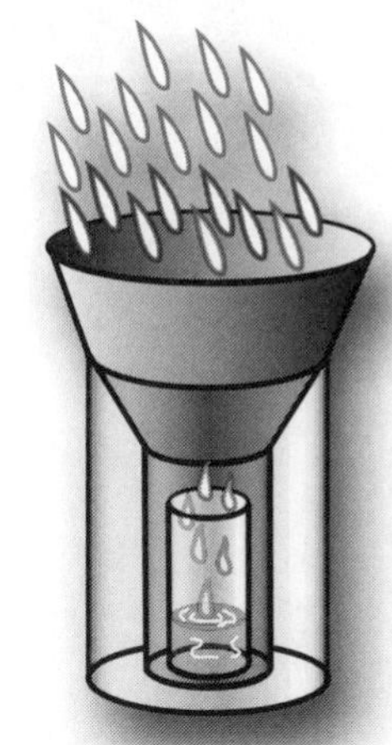

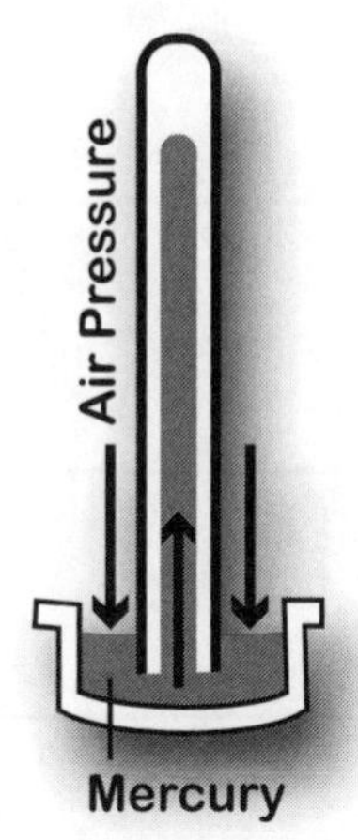

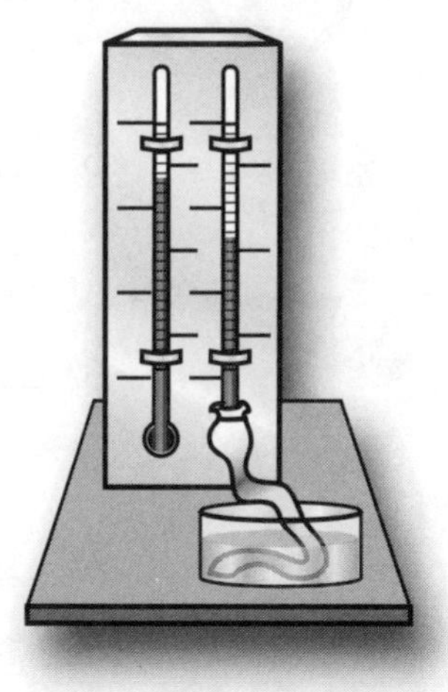

4. ____________________ 5. ____________________ 6. ____________________

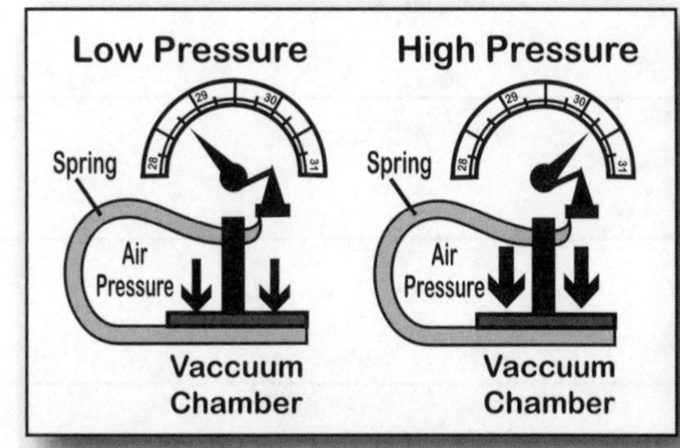

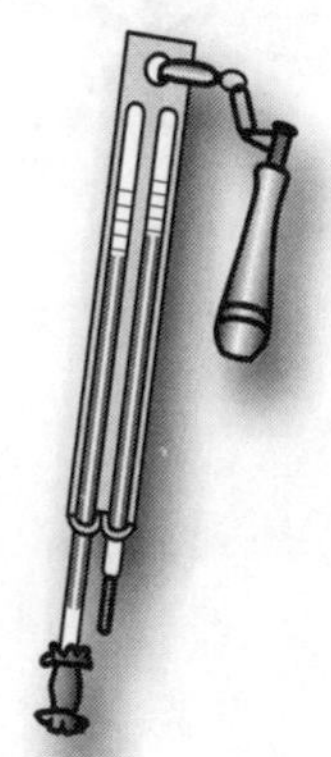

7. ____________________ 8. ____________________ 9. ____________________

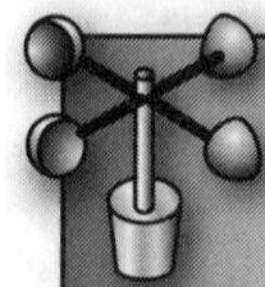

Meteorology Warm-ups: Weather Map Symbols

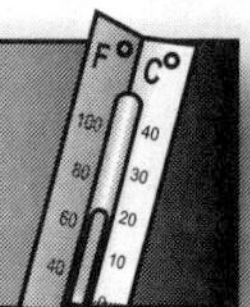

Label the symbols with the terms from Predicting the Weather 15 on page 25.

1. ______________________________
2. ______________________________
3. ______________________________
4. ______________________________
5. ______________________________
6. ______________________________
7. ______________________________
8. ______________________________
9. ______________________________
10. ______________________________
11. ______________________________

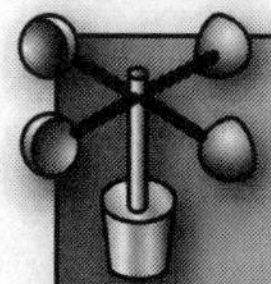

Meteorology Warm-ups: Weather Map

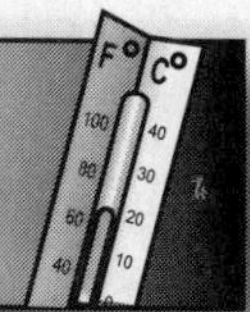

Use this map to answer the questions from Predicting the Weather 18 on page 26.

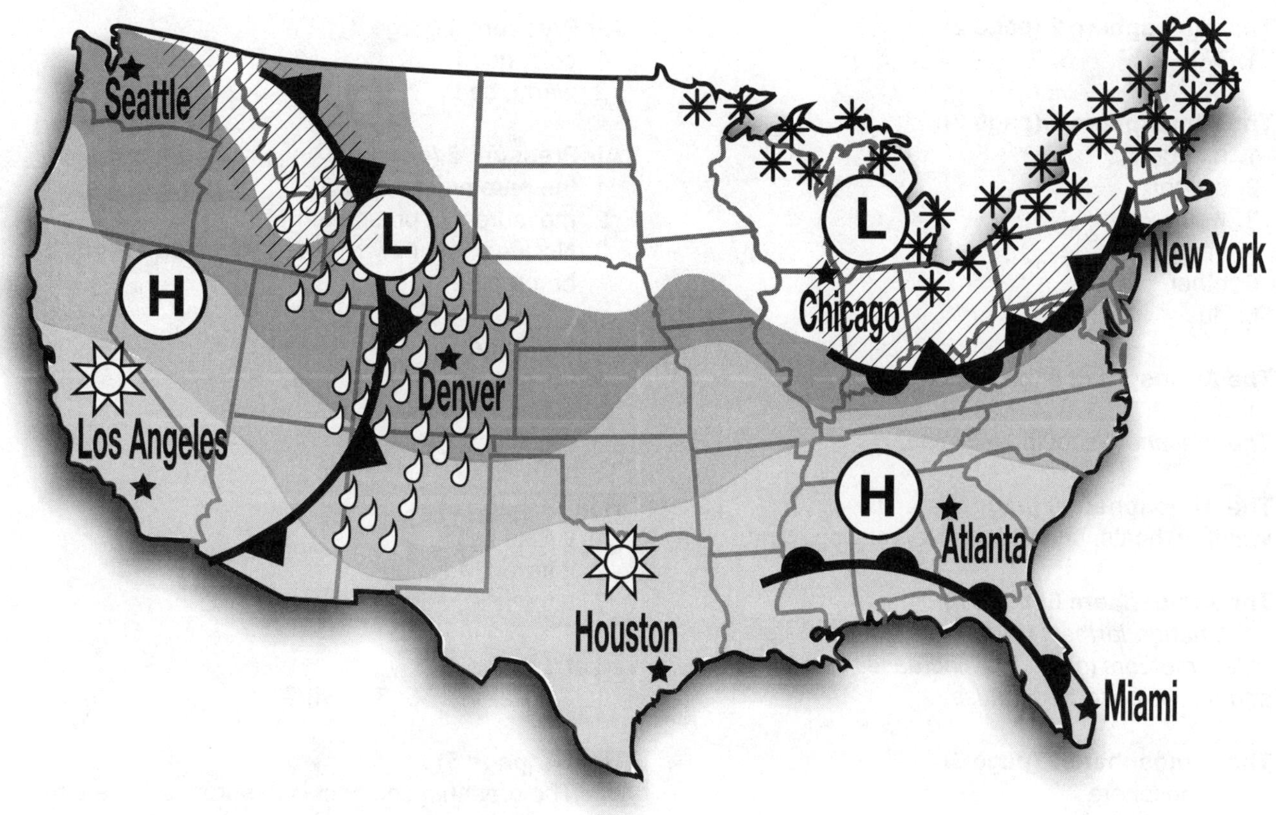

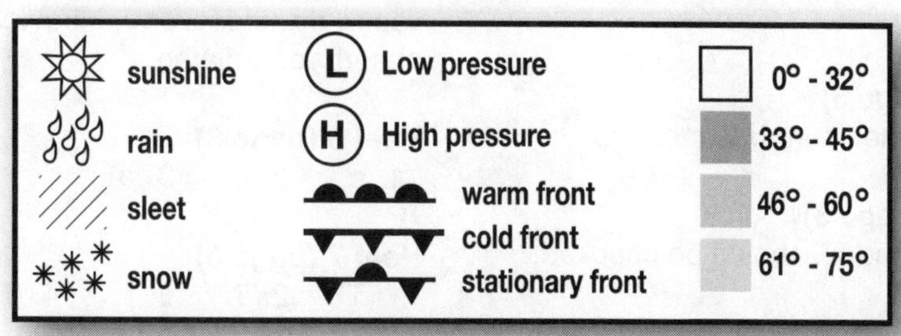

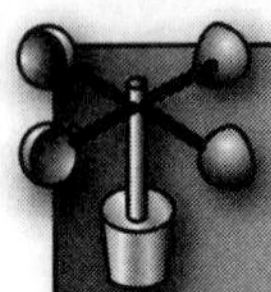

Meteorology Warm-ups: Answer Keys

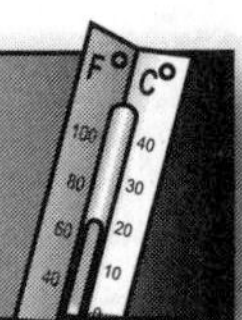

The Atmosphere 1 (page 2)

Answers will vary. One possibility is the layer of air that surrounds the earth and goes up 1,000 miles, made up of nitrogen, oxygen, water vapor, and other gases.

The Atmosphere 2 (page 2)

1. T 2. F 3. T 4. T 5. F

The Atmosphere 3 (page 2)

1. nitrogen
2. oxygen
3. water vapor
4. carbon dioxide
5. other gases
6. dust

The Atmosphere 4 (page 2)

1. 3 2. 1 3. 4 4. 2

Thermosphere should be circled.

The Atmosphere 5 (page 2)

Weather, heats, unevenly, move, rotation, wind

The Atmosphere 6 (page 3)

Change *farthest from* to *nearest to*, *meters* to *miles*, *meteors* to *weather*, *increases* to *decreases*, and *tropostop* to *tropopause.*

The Atmosphere 7 (page 3)

1. troposphere
2. ionosphere
3. stratosphere
4. mesosphere

The Atmosphere 8 (page 3)

stratosphere

The Atmosphere 9 (page 3)

mesosphere, winds, winter, summer, meteors

The Atmosphere 10 (page 3)

Sentences #2, #3, #4, and #5 should be checked.

Air Pressure 1 (page 4)

Gravity, earth, weight, pressure, amount, temperature

Air Pressure 2 (page 4)

1. No 2. Yes 3. Yes 4. Yes

Air Pressure 3 (page 4)

1. A beach at sea level
2. The equator
3. A cold, snowy day
4. The stratosphere

Air Pressure 4 (page 4)

1. cold, good
2. warm, bad

Air Pressure 5 (page 4)

1. the barometer
2. measures air pressure
3. No, we use a new type of barometer, the aneroid barometer.

Heat 1 (page 5)

1. the sun
2. electromagnetic
3. radiation

Heat 2 (page 5)

1. visible light
2. infrared radiation
3. ultraviolet radiation

Heat 3 (page 5)

1. T 2. F 3. T 4. T

Heat 4 (page 5)

The greenhouse effect is the process where the earth's surface, when heated, radiates some heat back into the atmosphere, and that heat gets trapped by the gases in the air, keeping the heat in.

Heat 5 (page 5)

vapor, dioxide, ozone, ultraviolet, reflected, scattered, absorbed, radiated

Heat 6 (page 6)

1. c 2. b 3. a

Heat 7 (page 6)

1. T 2. T 3. F 4. T

Heat 8 (page 6)

Sunlight strikes the equator at an angle close to 0 degrees. It is more efficient, brighter, and warmer. Near the poles, the sunlight strikes at nearly a 90-degree angle. It doesn't warm very efficiently, making temperatures colder.

Heat 9 (page 6)
molecules, dense, slow, sinks, rise, movement

Heat 10 (page 6)
1. F 2. C 3. F 4. F
5. F 6. C 7. C 8. C

Winds 1 (page 7)
1. air pressure
2. high, low
3. heating

Winds 2 (page 7)
Anemometer

Winds 3 (page 7)
1. coming from
2. from, to
3. higher, lower

Winds 4 (page 7)

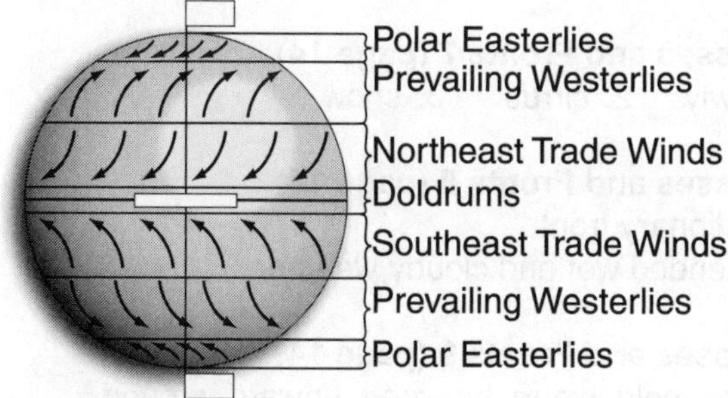

Winds 5 (page 7)
1. The Doldrums
2. Trade winds
3. Polar Easterlies
4. Prevailing Westerlies

Winds 6 (page 8)
The Coriolis Effect is how the earth's rotation makes the winds curve.

Winds 7 (page 8)
Sailors relied on these winds to sail across the ocean and carry their cargoes to participate in trade.

Winds 8 (page 8)
jet streams, high, west, east, time, fuel, slowed

Winds 9 (page 8)
1. T 2. F 3. T 4. T

Winds 10 (page 8)
Monsoon

Water in the Atmosphere 1 (page 9)
1. water vapor
2. rain, sleet
3. snow, hail, frost

Water in the Atmosphere 2 (page 9)
1. b 2. d 3. a 4. c

Water in the Atmosphere 3 (page 9)
1. oceans 2. puddles 3. leaves
4. streams 5. ponds 6. seas
7. soil 8. lakes

Water in the Atmosphere 4 (page 9)
The process of evaporation of sweat from the skin is what makes us feel cooler. On days with high humidity, the process slows down because there is more water in the air.

Water in the Atmosphere 5 (page 9)
less, water vapor, liquid, crystals, condensation, atmosphere

Water in the Atmosphere 6 (page 10)
1. c 2. b 3. a 4. d

Water in the Atmosphere 7 (page 10)

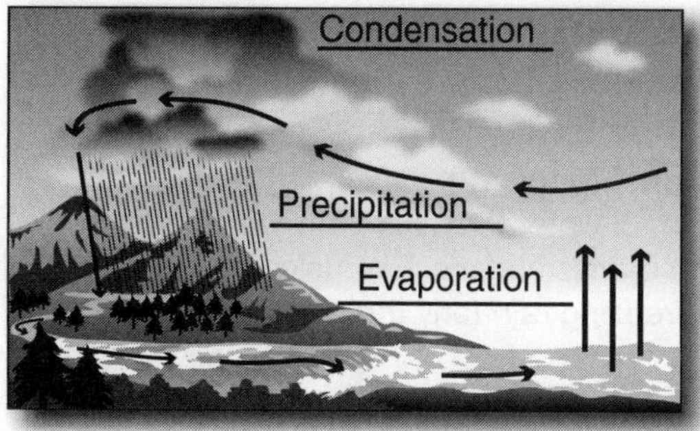

Water in the Atmosphere 8 (page 10)
1. Fog is clouds that form at or near the ground.
2. Fog dissipates when the sun evaporates the water droplets.

Water in the Atmosphere 9 (page 10)
Clouds form when water vapor molecules condense because the air has reached its dew point.

Water in the Atmosphere 10 (page 10)
mountain, upward, rises, cools, dew point, condense, clouds

Water in the Atmosphere 11 (page 11)

1. Cirrus 2. Cumulus
3. Stratus 4. Altostratus
5. Cirrocumulus 6. Altocumulus
7. Cumulonimbus 8. Nimbostratus

Water in the Atmosphere 12 (page 11)

1. c 2. d 3. a 4. b

Water in the Atmosphere 13 (page 11)

1. Cumulonimbus
2. Cirrus
3. Stratus
4. Nimbo- or Nimbus

Water in the Atmosphere 14 (page 11)

Virga, rain, super-dry, droplets, vapor, disappear

Water in the Atmosphere 15 (page 11)

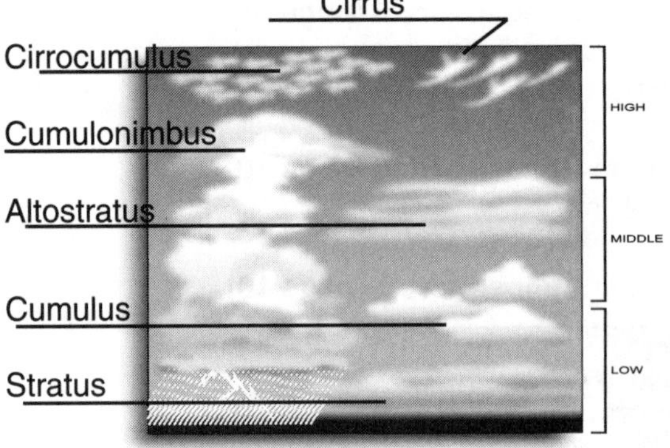

Precipitation 1 (page 12)

Any form of water that falls from the clouds and reaches the earth's surface. Examples: rain, snow, sleet, hail, freezing rain (any three)

Precipitation 2 (page 12)

1. T 2. F 3. F 4. T 5. F

Precipitation 3 (page 12)

1. e 2. d 3. a 4. b 5. c

Precipitation 4 (page 12)

1. rain
2. They reflect light.
3. a rain gauge

Precipitation 5 (page 12)

Hail, freeze, ice, travel, thunderclouds, heavy

Air Masses and Fronts 1 (page 13)

Pressure, Temperature, Humidity, Million

Air Masses and Fronts 2 (page 13)

1. air pressure
2. temperature
3. wind direction
4. moisture

Air Masses and Fronts 3 (page 13)

1. Tropical — forms over land; dry
2. Polar — forms over oceans; humid
3. Maritime — forms over the tropics; warm
4. Continental — cold; forms north or south of 50 degree latitudes

Air Masses and Fronts 4 (page 13)

1. T 2. T 3. T 4. F

Air Masses and Fronts 5 (page 13)

cold, warm, stationary, occluded (in any order)

Air Masses and Fronts 6 (page 14)

1. Yes 2. Yes 3. No 4. Yes

Air Masses and Fronts 7 (page 14)

1. slowly 2. cirrus 3. snow

Air Masses and Fronts 8 (page 14)

1. Stationary front
2. Extended wet and cloudy weather

Air Masses and Fronts 9 (page 14)

occluded, cold, warm, between, upward, ground

Air Masses and Fronts 10 (page 14)

1. AC 2. C

Storms 1 (page 15)

1. cumulonimbus 2. rises 3. heavy

Storms 2 (page 15)

updrafts, clouds, ground, spreads, burst, wind shear

Storms 3 (page 15)

Lightning

Storms 4 (page 15)

1. Thunder
2. Because light travels faster than sound.

Storms 5 (page 15)

Sentences #2, #3, and #5 should be checked.

Storms 6 (page 16)

Sheet lightning is from cloud to cloud, while fork lightning is from cloud to ground.

Storms 7 (page 16)

Change *cold* to *warm*, *downward* to *upward*, *rising* to *spinning*, *top* to *base* or *bottom*, and *trees* to *ground*.

Storms 8 (page 16)

1. 2 miles 2. 4 kilometers
3. The storm is moving away.

Storms 9 (page 16)

1. F 2. T 3. T 4. T

Storms 10 (page 16)

1. T 2. T 3. F 4. T

Storms 11 (page 17)

Tornado Alley is an area in the midwestern United States where tornadoes are more common than anywhere else in the world.

Storms 12 (page 17)

1. twister 2. waterspout 3. dust devil

Storms 13 (page 17)

1. 370 mph 2. A few minutes
3. Water is heavier than air.

Storms 14 (page 17)

1. b 2. c 3. a

Storms 15 (page 17)

Answers will vary.

Storms 16 (page 18)

1. T 2. T 3. F 4. T

Storms 17 (page 18)

1. c 2. b 3. a

Storms 18 (page 18)

hurricane, tropical, winds, low, spinning, land

Storms 19 (page 18)

a. 3 b. 4 c. 1 d. 2

Storms 20 (page 18)

1. lower, faster
2. lowest, warmest, center

Storms 21 (page 19)

1. semi-strong rain and winds
2. extremely strong wind, rain, and lightning
3. calm, clear skies

Storms 22 (page 19)

land, strength, slow, energy, water

Storms 23 (page 19)

1. A hurricane watch means hurricane conditions are possible in the next 36 hours. A hurricane warning means hurricane conditions are expected within the next 24 hours.
2. Answers will vary (evacuate, board up windows, get in the center of your building away from windows, store food and water, etc.).

Storms 24 (page 19)

In any order:

Satellites - help track storms visually
Hurricane hunters - fly over and/or into hurricanes to get data on wind speed, temperatures, etc.

Storms 25 (page 19)

A storm surge is a huge wall of water that hits the shore in a hurricane. It washes away beaches and structures and sometimes floods nearby areas.

Storms 26 (page 20)

cools, dry, water vapor, condenses, snow, lake effect

Storms 27 (page 20)

1. Yes 2. Yes 3. No 4. Yes

Storms 28 (page 20)

1. c 2. a 3. b 4. d

Storms 29 (page 20)

An avalanche

Storms 30 (page 20)

Answers will vary.

Weather Facts 1 (page 21)

1. drought
2. wildfires
3. dust storms

Information about each will vary.

Weather Facts 2 (page 21)

Rainbows, sunlight, bend, colors, circle

Weather Facts 3 (page 21)

1. red 2. orange 3. yellow 4. green
5. blue 6. indigo 7. violet

Weather Facts 4 (page 21)

1. fogbow 2. moonbow
3. rainbow 4. icebow

Weather Facts 5 (page 21)
Aurora (Borealis in the Northern Hemisphere, Australis in the Southern Hemisphere)

Weather Facts 6 (page 22)
Pacific, South America, humid, rains, El Niño

Weather Facts 7 (page 22)
All of the items should be circled except *high waves.*

Weather Facts 8 (page 22)
1. b 2. a 3. c

Weather Facts 9 (page 22)
The job of the ozone layer is to absorb ultraviolet rays, and shields the earth from their harmful effects.

Weather Facts 10 (page 22)
1. T 2. T 3. T 4. F 5. T

Predicting the Weather 1 (page 23)
1. F 2. T 3. F 4. T 5. T

Predicting the Weather 2 (page 23)
1. Air pressure
2. Humidity
3. Temperature

Predicting the Weather 3 (page 23)

1. barometer	temperature
2. psychrometer	wind speed
3. thermometer	relative humidity
4. anemometer	wind direction
5. wind vane	air pressure

Predicting the Weather 4 (page 23)
They take photos of Earth's weather. They can track hurricanes and provide information to meteorologists about clouds, storms, and ice and snow cover.

Predicting the Weather 5 (page 23)
buoys, data, satellites, tracking, currents

Predicting the Weather 6 (page 24)
Any four of these: weather balloons, weather stations, satellites, local weather observers, radar, the National Weather Service, computers

Predicting the Weather 7 (page 24)
Radar

Predicting the Weather 8 (page 24)
1. anemometer 2. weather balloon
3. wind vane 4. rain gauge
5. mercury barometer 6. hygrometer
7. thermometer 8. aneroid barometer
9. psychrometer

Predicting the Weather 9 (page 24)
supercomputers, analyze, space, millions, predict

Predicting the Weather 10 (page 24)
Because the oceans greatly influence the earth's climate.

Predicting the Weather 11 (page 25)
1. Yes 2. Yes 3. Yes 4. No

Predicting the Weather 12 (page 25)
Any four of the following: weather systems, fronts, temperature, precipitation, cloud cover, wind speed, lightning strikes, water vapor

Predicting the Weather 13 (page 25)
An isobar is a line that connects points of equal air pressure, while an isotherm is a line that connects points of equal air temperature.

Predicting the Weather 14 (page 25)

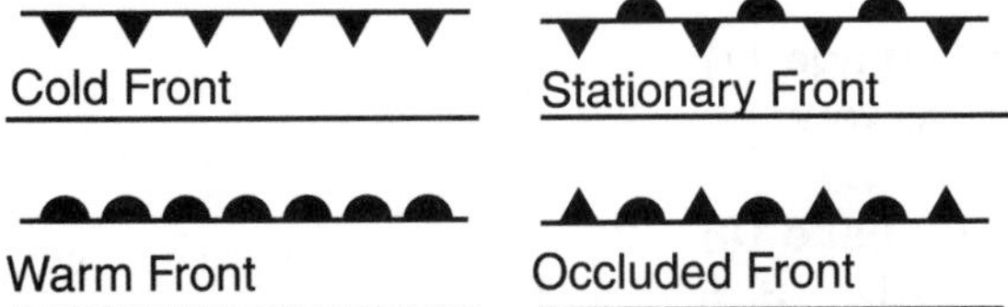

Predicting the Weather 15 (page 25)
1. drizzle
2. fog
3. hail
4. haze
5. rain
6 shower
7. sleet
8. smoke
9. snow
10. thunderstorm
11. hurricane

Predicting the Weather 16 (page 26)
1. c 2. a 3. b

Predicting the Weather 17 (page 26)
temperatures, cloud, precipitation, fronts, pressure

Predicting the Weather 18 (page 26)
1. Rain
2. Los Angeles or Atlanta
3. Denver or Chicago
4. three
5. Winter, because there is snow

Predicting the Weather 19 (page 26)
Answers will vary.

Predicting the Weather 20 (page 26)
1. synoptic charts
2. So that meteorologists anywhere in the world, regardless of what language they speak, can read the information; to save space

Weather Myths and Folklore 1 (page 27)

1. Clear moon,	a year of plenty.
2. Red sky at night,	the nearer the rain.
3. Red sky in morning,	frost soon.
4. Rainbow in morning	sailor take warning.
5. A year of snow,	sailor's delight.
6. The farther the sight,	gives you fair warning.

Weather Myths and Folklore 2 (page 27)
1. F 2. F 3. F 4. F

Weather Myths and Folklore 3 (page 27)
1. Thor
2. Ra
3. Huracan
4. Poseidon

Weather Myths and Folklore 4 (page 27)
Humid, damp air usually precedes a storm.

Weather Myths and Folklore 5 (page 27)
1. cows
2. thunderstorm
3. squirrel's
4. red
5. ring

Climate 1 (page 28)
Answers will vary. One possibility: The average weather conditions over many years of a particular area are its climate.

Climate 2 (page 28)
temperature, precipitation

Climate 3 (page 28)
1. latitude
2. altitude
3. distance from large bodies of water
4. ocean currents

Climate 4 (page 28)
Tropical-warm
Temperate-varied warm and cold
Polar-cold

Climate 5 (page 28)
temperature, mountains, altitude, cooler, tropical

Climate 6 (page 29)
1. less 2. more 3. mild

Climate 7 (page 29)
currents, tropics, poles, equator, land

Climate 8 (page 29)
Any two of the following: air masses, nearness to bodies of water, landforms, latitude

Climate 9 (page 29)
1. prevailing winds
2. water vapor
3. warm

Climate 10 (page 29)
Marine climates
Cool summers
Warm winters
Coastal areas
Less temperature variation

Continental climates
Hot summers
Cold winters
Inland areas
More temperature variation

Climate 11 (page 30)
Sahara, Mediterranean, Atlantic, dry, toward, Asia

Climate 12 (page 30)
1. windward
2. cools, condenses
3. dry

Climate 13 (page 30)

A microclimate is a small area with specific climate conditions that has its own weather (often somewhat different from the regular climate of the surrounding region).

Climate 14 (page 30)

1. tilt, axis 2. North Star 3. day (24 hours)

Climate 15 (page 30)

1. T 2. T 3. F 4. T

Climate 16 (page 31)

1. Tropical
2. Dry
3. Temperate Marine
4. Temperate Continental
5. Polar

Climate 17 (page 31)

1. Rain Forest
2. Rains every day, hot and humid, lush vegetation
3. rains, afternoon

Climate 18 (page 31)

1. A tropical wet-and-dry climate gets slightly less rain than a tropical wet climate, and it has distinct wet and dry seasons. Instead of rain forests, there are savannas.
2. equator

Climate 19 (page 31)

precipitation, evaporate, dry, rainfall, hotter

Climate 20 (page 31)

Tropical:

Tropical wet
Tropical wet-and-dry

Dry:

Arid
Semiarid

Temperate Marine:

Marine west coast
Mediterranean
Humid subtropical

Temperate Continental:

Humid continental
Subarctic

Polar:

Tundra
Ice cap

Climate 21 (page 32)

1. F 2. T 3. T 4. F 5. T

Climate 22 (page 32)

1. Chihuahuan Desert
2. Great Basin Desert
3. Mojave Desert
4. Sonoran Desert

Climate 23 (page 32)

1. Many short grasses grow there, which is perfect for grazing animals.
2. wheat, oats, corn, sunflowers, etc. (any two)

Climate 24 (page 32)

1. b 2. a 3. c

Climate 25 (page 32)

1. Mediterranean
2. Humid subtropical
3. Marine west coast

Climate 26 (page 33)

1. T 2. T 3. F 4. T

Climate 27 (page 33)

1. b 2. a

Climate 28 (page 33)

tundra, Canada, cold, cool, permafrost, trees, animals

Climate 29 (page 33)

Polar or Ice cap

Climate 30 (page 33)

1. c 2. a 3. b